BEYOND *the*
UNTHINKABLE

BY
CYNTHIA PORTARO

CYN'SATIONAL PUBLISHING

Karen Yelverton
5.0 out of 5 stars
Book of Hope
There is no way I can even judge or rate a book that comes from so deep within a human soul and unimaginable life experiences. I could not put this book down. It is impossible to imagine walking in her footsteps but she allows us to walk beside her helping her readers see how she found her way out of what must have felt like a living hell none of which she asked for. She helps light the way back to a life from a deep pit of utter despair and pure agony to ultimate freedom, pure love and true wisdom. This book is for everyone. When we don't know what to say or a little of how tragedy may feel this book will give you tremendous insight you never knew you would desperately need someday. Thank you Cynthia for becoming such an instrument of God's peace and love to a world of people that seem to be losing hope. At a time when so many feel hopeless you will find so much hope here. Such an amazing tribute to honor her children and Jesus Christ.

Patricia Thomas
5.0 out of 5 stars
A Must Read!
I gave this book a 5 star because it was hard to put it down! It helps those who have gone through traumatic events and also those who haven't experienced any all. For those who have gone through painful traumatic events and need further healing, this Christian book will be a blessing and is a must read! For those who haven't, you will learn how to minister to those who have and gain a wealth of knowledge on what not to do or say and how to be the support that is needed

at the time. I want to thank the author for writing this gut wrenching book because I know it wasn't easy! Thanks for increasing my understanding of how to better minister to those facing devastating events in their lives!

Mary Rendina
5.0 out of 5 stars
<u>A powerful story of the healing and restorative power of God.</u>
Not many people would have the courage and strength to survive "The Unthinkable" let alone write about the experience in an effort to help others who are on the same journey. Cynthia Portaro's authentic, transparent and heartfelt story of surviving the loss of her children and then husband leaves the reader with a longing to have the level of faith and trust in God that she possesses. I would highly recommend you buy two of this book and gift it to someone who may be going through the grieving process. It truly gives hope to the hopeless.

Nancy Sandahl
5.0 out of 5 stars
<u>An Absolute to Read for Everyone!</u>
The Spirit of God radiates through Cynthia Portaro in her writing this book. Her honest and down to earth reflections on what she's had to journey through is amazing. This is a book that everyone should read, whether they've been through grief or not. How she has been able to turn something so hurting around to reaching out to others only reflects a true loving God. His Love is so overwhelming in this writing; no one should miss reading it. Thank you Cynthia for going that extra mile, even when you've been in pain!

DEDICATION

This true story is dedicated in memory of my two precious children, Michael Alano "Mikey P" and Christina Nicole "Chrissy P", who will, forever, remain in my soul. And, for those sons and daughters that were taken too soon, and especially their parents, who have become some of my dearest friends.

To my family, who have truly been there for me, during life's most difficult trials. First, my mother, Joan; my husband, Richard; and our surviving children, Maressa, Rico, Joseph, Kellie, and our grandchildren ... my joys, Braden, Brenna and Briley.

And, to the friends, who are more family than imaginable, and have stuck closer than a brother, always there to encourage me to write this season of overcoming and for keeping our family close in prayer.

Theresa & Richard, Rita, Pastor Jimmy, Mary Jo, Priscilla & Kevin, Mark and Jackie, Darlene, Kimmy, Kimberly M, Susan, Kelly, Laura, Donna S, Donna B, Jill, Pastors Paul & Denise, Jim & Joan, Chris, Rick & Dez, Robyn, Doris, Momma L, Vicky, Leslie, Ken, Karen, Don & Lorie, Hearts of Prayer Team, International Church of Las Vegas, Faith Lutheran Junior/Senior High School, The Las Vegas Metro Police Department, all of my children's friends and families ... and so many more. Also, to those who have done so much for our family during tumultuous times, either prayed, donated or shown simple 'Acts of Kindness.'

From the bottom of our hearts, we thank you.

"... And above all these things put on charity, which is the bond of perfection." Colossians 3:14 NIV

And let the peace of Christ rule in your hearts, to which indeed you were called in one body. And be thankful. Let the word of Christ dwell in you richly, teaching and admonishing one another in all wisdom, singing psalms and hymns and spiritual songs, with thankfulness in your hearts to God. And whatever you do, in word or deed, do everything in the name of the Lord Jesus, giving thanks to God the Father through him.
Colossians 3:15-17

Amber Marie Santor
September 29, 1983 - October 3, 2019

This page is dedicated to the entire Santor family and my best friends
Richard and Theresa Hollowell. Who are grieving the loss of their daughter, their sister,
their niece, their aunt and their friend.
My heart goes out to everyone who is missing this precious child.

She's in the sun, the wind, the rain.
She's in the air you breathe with every breath you take.
She sings a song of hope and cheer, where there is no more pain or fear.
You'll see her in the clouds above, hear her whisper words of love.
You'll be together before long, until then listen for her song.

INTRODUCTION: THE BLINK OF AN EYE

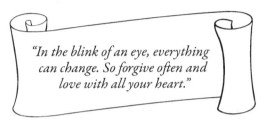

"In the blink of an eye, everything can change. So forgive often and love with all your heart."

"Measured against eternity, our time on earth is just a blink of an eye, but the consequences of it will last forever." Rick Warren

I imagine some of you reading this story might think, while reading through the chapters, "This has to be fictional, this story is unreal." To be honest, I wish it were a fictional novel. However, unfortunately, for my family, it is very true to the core. I feel it and live with this truth every single day of my life. Though not without our Lord and Savior leaving footprints in the sand as He carried me through the days. I just had to trust him to handle every piece of my shattered heart and catch every tear that has been shed throughout the years.

"For the Lamb at the center of the throne will be the shepherd; He will lead them to springs of living water. And God will wipe away every tear from their eyes." Revelation 7:17 NIV

That "BLINK" for our family occurred on March 30, 2011, when life ended for our son, Michael, at *22 years, 10 months and 5 days of age.* Right then and there in the "blink of an eye", life changed forever. Unfortunately, the blink turned into a lightning storm of flashes as tragedy struck our family over and over. We drifted through the storm of events like a tiny sailboat under the dark shadow of mountain-like waves.

Michael's death led me to think more about Christ's life. God gave His only begotten Son, Jesus, so we may have life everlasting. I was thankful for that sacrifice but often found myself selfishly wanting my son back as I cried out, "But Lord, I am not that strong like You!"

Little did I know, at that time, how much I would learn.

Through these tidal waves of events that slammed my family, one after another, the Lord took me into deeper places I never knew existed in His world. First, it began with the life of His Apostle Paul. Paul's example of true suffering is found numerous times throughout the New Testament.

He taught me what Paul meant by those words suffering, hope, patience, character and glory. He states again and again of our own weaknesses and how our inner self is being renewed day by day to glorify God. In the book of *2 Corinthians ESV*, Paul shares the message of the relationship between suffering, and the power of the Holy Spirit. *"Out of suffering will come new life, ministries and a very powerful message of hope." "Though our outer self is wasting away, our inner self is being renewed day-by-day."* This is when God's light will shine in our darkest hours. It certainly is not an easy road, if you choose to follow it. The daily battle is to decide how to trust "God" in your walk of Hope and Victory in those most difficult moments. One question, over these past years, for me has been, "Lord how are you going to use this to glorify You and honor the lives of my children?" Paul said, our tragedy will minister to those in need of healing ... starting in verse one ...

"Therefore, having this ministry by the mercy of God, we do not lose heart. 2 But we have renounced disgraceful, underhanded ways. We refuse to practice cunning or to tamper with God's word, but by the open statement of the truth we would commend ourselves to everyone's conscience in the sight of God. 3 And even if our gospel is veiled, it is veiled to those who are perishing. 4 In their case the god of this world has blinded the minds of the unbelievers, to keep them from seeing the light of the gospel of the glory of Christ, who is the image of God. 5 For what we proclaim is not ourselves, but Jesus Christ as Lord, with ourselves as your servants for Jesus' sake. 6 For God, who said, "Let light shine out of darkness has shone in our hearts to give the light of the knowledge of the glory of God in the face of Jesus Christ."

Paul, again and again, tells us the weakness of his life is designed to magnify the power of God's name. The strong words of his letter in *Chapter 4:7-12*, he speaks about the purpose of his suffering. "You mean there is going to be a purpose in this suffering?"

7 But we have this treasure in jars of clay, to show that the surpassing power belongs to God and not to us. 8 We are afflicted in every way, but not crushed; perplexed, but not driven to despair; 9 persecuted, but not forsaken; struck down, but not destroyed; 10 always carrying in the body the death of Jesus, so that the life of Jesus may also be manifested in our bodies. 11 For we who live are always being given over to death for Jesus' sake, so that the life of Jesus also may be manifested in our mortal flesh. 12 So death is at work in us, but life in you.

Paul's words in verses 13–18 is where our HOPE originates. Hope is putting Faith to work, when doubting would be easier. This is the place where I found strength to barely roll out of bed.

Through my very own personal daily trials, grieving heart and soul, I would find my place to help change the way the world has seen death and at its worst possible moment in time.

13 "Since we have the same spirit of faith according to what has been written, "I believed, and so I spoke," we also believe, and so we also speak, 14 knowing that He who raised the Lord Jesus will raise us also with Jesus and bring us with you into his presence. 15 For it is all for your sake, so that as grace extends to more and more people it may increase thanksgiving, to the glory of God."

16 "So we do not lose heart. Though our outer self is wasting away, our inner self is being renewed day by day. 17 For this light momentary affliction is preparing for us an eternal weight of glory beyond all comparison, 18 as we look not to the things that are seen but to the things that are unseen. For the things that are seen are transient, but the things that are unseen are eternal."

It took me nine years to finally agree with God and write our story. Digging into the memories of the pain endured has been very trying on my heart and soul. Making a promise to God and then apparently forgetting to actually follow through is not something He will allow. Thankfully, I have been journaling dating back to 1982, and I have many written memories of these past nine years documented, along with multiple dreams and visions of fulfilling my promise to Him done ... not only to honor God but to also honor the lives of my children. Brandon J. Hill may have killed Mikey's body, but his blood will still speak through me to help others endure the journey of brokenness.

Incredible organizations have originated out of pain and suffering. A few that come to mind are MADD, Mothers of

Murdered Children, Adams Place, etc. There are thousands of reasons we can do the same. Our loved ones who leave us don't have to be distant memories or a stone in the grass. Choose to keep them alive by continuing the work they were passionate about, no matter how painful life may be without them.

Their memory and spirits will live on!

"And the God of all grace, who called you to his eternal glory in Christ, after you have suffered a little while, will himself restore you and make you strong, firm and steadfast." 1 Peter 5:10 NIV

As Christians, we believe God is a God of restoration. We also know our children or loved ones are not coming back to earth. As much as we would love for that to happen, this will not take place until we are reunited in Heaven. However, I do believe, He will restore our hearts and lives in a powerful way, which will bring peace that surpasses all our understanding but ... in a much different way.

"Don't fret or worry. Instead of worrying, pray. Let petitions and praises shape your worries into prayers, letting God know your concerns. Before you know it, a sense of God's wholeness, everything coming together for good, will come and settle you down. It's wonderful what happens when Christ displaces worry at the center of your life." Philippians 4:6-7 (MSG)

I pray my story and tragedies will bless you with a deeper and more powerful relationship with our Savior, Jesus Christ ... the only one true friend, who heals, and gives hope during these seasons of life that will turn us upside down and inside out, as we continue our walk, in faith, to honor those taken too soon.

This is my prayer for you.

That Feeling you get
In your Stomach,
When your Heart's Broken.
It's Like all the
Butterflies just died.

Chapter 1

THE DEVASTATION

Merriam Webster's dictionary defines "killer" as *"one that has a forceful, violent, or striking impact"*.[1]

triking impact makes it sound like a single, isolated incident that ends after the killer's actions. While a killer's actions may only last a moment, I can attest to the fact that the effects continue on throughout the lifetime of their victim's surviving relatives and lifelong friends.

"A person, animal, or thing that kills, murderer, assassin, slaughterer, butcher, serial killer, gunman, executioner, hit man, cutthroat, literary, slayer, a major killer." If just reading these synonyms of *killer* intensifies the injustice...imagine living through the actual act of the brutality.

What has to go through a person's mind to say, "I don't want him breathing anymore?" What makes someone so entitled to make the decision to take someone's breath away? What makes a person so hollow they live in such a dark place and commit such a vicious crime?

Those are some of the thoughts I struggled with after the fact. But, I'm getting a little ahead of myself. Let's go back to the beginning of this story.

Ever since Mikey was young, he loved performing on any stage, either at school plays or in front of his family and friends. I have a photo of him at about eight years old, rapping

---

[1] https://www.merriam-webster.com/dictionary/killer

and dancing in a Shephard's outfit. He was always really into improving his skills, which included vocals, amazing dance moves, and writing lyrics. There wasn't a hateful bone in his body. Why would anyone want to take his life? He was such a fun, loving, easy-going guy.

Mikey and I worked together. We were at the Mirage Hotel this particular day. He was in such an incredibly great mood and excited for the concert he and his partner, Jeff, were performing the following Thursday evening. He asked me, around 2 p.m., if he could leave work early to sell tickets for the show. Of course, I said, "Sure."

He handed me four tickets with an extremely big smile, staring at me with those big baby blues, as he said, "That will be $64.00, Mom."

His very first sale of the day; ... which, I was more than happy to purchase. I handed him a $100 bill, and was pleased to tell him, as usual, "Keep the change, Love Bug, for gas and food." He hugged me with a tight grizzly bear hug, as he always did. While holding me close, he told me he was going to sing the song he had written especially for me at the concert. My heart and soul rejoiced as any proud Mom's would. He knew how to melt my spirit and fill my heart with so much love and joy.

That evening our lives changed forever happened when I was awakened by our dogs barking loudly, running in circles around my bedroom. The volume of their barks woke me from a deep sound sleep. "Did Mikey forget his key again?" I thought. Looking at the clock, it was 3:30 a.m. Yep, that would be like Mikey.

However, with that 3:30 a.m. knock on the door, I'd soon learn Mikey's special song for me was never going to be sung.

I approached the front door and looked out the window, it was a man in a police uniform, and a woman I could not identify. I spoke through the door, uncertain and not very awake. "What is going on?"

"Please open the door, Mrs. Portaro. We need to speak to you." The officer showed me his badge through the window, proving his identity.

As I opened the door, my heart pounded rapidly with fear of what they could possibly be doing at my front door so early in the morning. In a split second, thoughts ran through my mind, thinking of who could it be. I was informed enough to know police only come directly to your home when it's something fatal. My husband, Richard, was away on business, Mikey was obviously still out for the night, and our youngest son, Joey, was at Catalina Island for a senior class high school science trip. Rico, our oldest son, was asleep upstairs and Chrissy, our youngest, was there hovering over the staircase, wondering what was happening.

Before the door was fully opened, the words tumbled out of my mouth, "Who is it?"

"May we please come in and sit down?" the officer asked.

"No, tell me," I demanded, still blocking their entrance to the house, "I know you only come if it's fatal."

"It's Michael."

"What? What happened? Was he in an accident? Where is he?" My head began to spin, as I wondered if Mikey was alive, in some hospital alone, or worse, dead. "Tell me!"

"Please allow us to come in, Mrs. Portaro." The officer requested, again, calmly.

I obliged and walked them into the living room. The officer sat on the fireplace hearth, along with the woman. Chrissy and Rico, now *both* awake from my yelling, came into the living room to join me. We all sat on the sofa, directly across from the officers. Tears were running down my face and my heart began pounding out of my chest, as if I were having a massive coronary.

I kept thinking, "*This is a nightmare. I am not awake.*" Finally, I demanded, "Tell me, now!"

The officer spoke these words, as compassionately as I am sure he could, "Michael is dead."

I cannot even begin to explain the paralyzing effect those words had as terror gripped my heart. I could see the officer's lips were still moving, but my ears were no longer registering the audio. Chrissy and Rico were sitting next to me, but I could not feel their presence. They seemed to be questioning the officers, but I could no longer hear what they were saying. Thinking back, I believe they were sobbing, but even that was oblivious to me through the dark fog settled in my soul.

"Are you sure it's Mikey? Are you certain it's my son? It can't be!"

"This is not true. Please tell me, it's not true!"

"I was with him for most of the day."

"We've worked together every day for more than a year... this is impossible."

4

"I just spoke to him a few hours ago. He asked me if he could leave work early to go sell tickets to the concert, where he'll be performing tomorrow night."

Then, the inevitable happened, right there in front of me. The officer handed me Mikey's Driver's License, and told us he had been shot to death.

"Do you know if Michael was selling drugs?" the officer asked.

"What? What? What?" That seemed to be all I could utter out of my mouth. I wondered how the officer could even question me on such a thing. "No, he did not sell drugs! Why are you asking me this?

"The video surveillance shows Michael walking up to a white vehicle then exchanged something for money."

"He was out yesterday afternoon selling concert tickets ... not drugs. I saw him on his way out, as I was coming up our street. He was leaving our house, and we both stopped to talk for a few minutes. The last thing he said to me was, 'Thanks Mom, for letting me leave work early. I love you, you're the best'."

"Then, that explains that." The officer replied, "Do you know why anyone would want to kill your son?"

"Kill Mikey? NO!" *How could he suggest that there would be a reason?* "NO! NO! NO! NO! NO!" I wailed.

There is not much rationality when you're struck by the violent news that your baby has been shot to his death. I do not remember all of the conversation with the detectives. I do remember the woman finally introduced herself as, "The

Coroner." The sound of that word, *coroner*, made my body go limp and collapse to the floor sobbing. "Michael! Michael! My baby!"

For them, there was a dead body and a killer on the loose. It was their job to ask questions and get answers. But, I wanted them to stop talking. Every detail spoken about this abominable news felt like a poisonous arrow piercing my heart. Shock increased and my body began to shut down. All I could do was to continue calling out Mikey's name over and over.

"Michael! Michael! My baby!"

Wherever he was, I needed him to hear me! As the pain tormented through my body, I began to regain my thoughts and become more aware of my surroundings. Aware of the other children still in the room with me. I looked at my son, Rico.

"Mom," he choked out softly, "We better call Dad."

As I mentioned earlier, my husband, Richard, was away on business. He was not answering his phone, apparently sound asleep in his hotel room. I suppose that's something to be expected at 4:30 a.m. in the morning, but not something you process when you've just received shocking news. After many failed attempts to reach Richard on his cell phone, we finally decided to contact the local police in the town where he was staying. They went to the hotel, knocked on his door, and delivered the same shocking news. Although I felt lost and alone when I received the news, I still had two of my children with me when the officers left the house. I cannot imagine the agony Richard experienced on the three-hour drive home. He later admitted to crying hysterically, while attempting to get back to the house as quickly and safely as possible. When he finally arrived, we revealed all the details of the brutal truth of Mikey's senseless murder.

Sometime, right before Richard arrived, I think maybe around 7 a.m., I realized our youngest son, Joey, was on his senior class trip to Catalina Island, California. Because Joey's birthday is April 1, I had planned to have some friends bring him gifts and balloons from us to celebrate, even though we couldn't be together for his special day. Unfortunately, that surprise never happened. Instead it turned into the school principal pulling Joey out and telling him the news of his brother.

I phoned my best friend, who's as close as a sister, Theresa, and her husband, Richard, who live in Newport Beach, California, and who are my children's GodParents. They willingly, and sacrificially, flew Joey home during all the chaos.

Most of these details have been retold to me by family and friends, because I do not personally remember much of this nightmarish morning. I remember the police coming to the door and the initial shock, but during the hours that followed, my mind must have switched to an auto-pilot mode, forcing my body to go through simple motions. I remember making a few calls, screaming to my mother, family, and very limited friends that Mikey had been murdered. But, everything else is a blur or fogginess. My son had been murdered!

Many of our best friends, neighbors, and other extended family came to be with us. Before we knew it, our home was filled with what I remember to be hundreds of people carrying food, cases of drinks, and whatever else you bring to "the" party. Then came the reporters and news crews, with even more people everywhere.

They wanted to be there for us and show their condolences and love. But, the arrival of every new person felt suffocating. *Thank you for your love, thank you for your condolences, but I don't want any of this. I just want Mikey.* I thought over and over. *Why my son? Why such a brutal death?*

The visitors became fewer and fewer, but the suffocating nightmares continued on every single night for months on end. All I could do was lie in bed, thinking of my son lying on a cold cemented parking lot, in a pool of his own blood, alone, cold and dead. Shot multiple times, execution style, with one final shot to the head. He lied there for 10 minutes, before someone found his dead, lifeless body. A sign directly across the street, with bright lights shining ***EMERGENCY ROOM***! How does that happen? One of our city's largest hospitals within walking distance and not one passerby saw a dead young man's body.

When a future is robbed from your life,
especially from another's bad choice ...
it just makes the root of the pain much stronger and deeper.

I couldn't personally take any more of this, so I retreated to my bedroom to be alone and cry out to God...

"Why? Why? Why?"

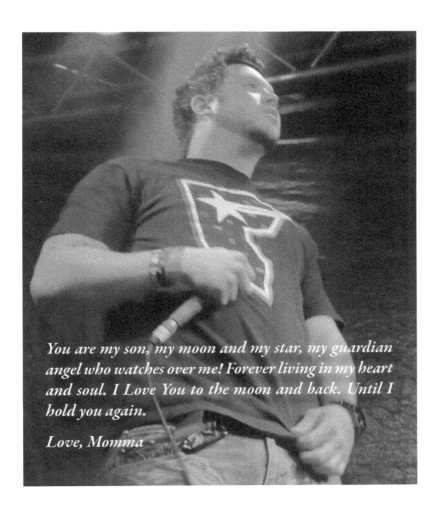

You are my son, my moon and my star, my guardian angel who watches over me! Forever living in my heart and soul. I Love You to the moon and back. Until I hold you again.

Love, Momma

Chapter 2

Michael Alano Portaro

"Mikey P"
(May 25, 1988- March 30, 2011)

"Love your enemies, do good to them, and lend to them without expecting to get anything back. Then your reward will be great, and you will be children of the Most High, because he is kind to the ungrateful and wicked." Luke 6:35 NIV

My family faced so much destruction through the tormenting shock of Mikey's death. For over two months, we were continually bombarded with daily news reports from local TV stations and front-page articles in local newspapers, with updates on the search for Mikey's killer. I recall sitting at the airport, waiting for a flight, when Mikey's beautiful face flashed on the large TV screen hanging in the waiting area. As I sat frozen, my life flashing before my eyes, a gentleman sitting next to me said, "That poor kid, and his family, how sad."

10

With all the strength in my soul, and tear drops sliding down my cheeks, I simply muttered out softly, "Yes, it's more than sad to our family. He is my son."

As I continued studying the life of Apostle Paul, I realized he was a man designed for leadership and friendship. He was compassionate and tender, yet blunt and to the point. I began to realize many similarities between Apostle Paul and Mikey. Though his time here on earth was brief, Mikey positively impacted the lives of everyone he encountered. His heart was gentle, tender, and trusting. His soul was designed for friendship and leadership. He had a heart that could expand and embrace the entire human family. Mikey would make any stranger in a room feel welcomed and safe. You realize this is true, when 1,200 people show up for his memorial service, and more than 600 watched it online. It is a testimony of the power of love given in his short, limited lifetime. Being able to call him "my son" makes me the proudest mother in the world.

Andy was one of Mikey's dearest friends. I could write an entire book devoted to their friendship. Andy was born with Arthrogryposis Multiplex Congenital. Because of this, Andy has lived his entire life in a wheelchair.

Mikey and Andy met in the seventh grade, when Andy's wheelchair accidentally bumped into Mikey. Andy shared with me, when this happened, he was gripped with fear. Most kids avoided looking at Andy and wouldn't even attempt to talk to him. Mikey turned around and, after seeing what had bumped into him, looked Andy right in the eye, smiled from ear to ear, and said, "Yo Dude, nice ride."

From that day forward, they became instant best friends, which led to many amazing stories of how Mikey took care of Andy, in and out of school. I remember walking into our house one day and Mikey had Andy's back on his back. My son, Joey, was holding Andy's feet as they headed up the stairs.

In total shock, I said, "What are you guys doing?"

Joey replied, "Andy wanted to see Mikey's room, Mom."

My eyes must have rolled in many different directions, while laughing, as I watched them tackle this endeavor. It was only one flight of stairs, but Andy wasn't exactly light. I thought how endearing and thoughtful it was for them to take on the task, since Andy was only able to imagine what Mikey's room looked like.

Some of these memories were shared from Mikey's friends in letters we received after the funeral, and they would have scared the life out of me if I had known the unusual, humorous antics Mikey chose to use with developing trusting relationships. This does not surprise me at all, though, because Mikey was always an active and mischievous kid.

The following letter is from Andy's parents and it was given to me after Mikey was killed. It has become one of my greatest treasures as to how he lived his life for others.

Dear Portaro's

The more than ten years Mike was in Andy's life could only be described as the best of times for our son. When Andy started school at Faith in sixth grade, he was a lonely little boy, who neither had friends nor knew how to make them. He would say "people just don't know what to do with me." Being different was awkward for everyone. He never fit in and was usually painfully teased at times.

Then, there came Mike. Andy was so surprised that this good-looking, popular athlete would even notice him, much less befriend him. From the day they met, Andy's life began. Mikey P always had Andy's back. If anyone ever gave Andy a bad time, Mike would step in and tell them if they had a problem with Andy they would have to go through him first ... problem solved.

For the next decade or so, Mike helped Andy live. Really live. He was his ambassador of fun, never letting Andy's limitations stop them from having a good time. There are so many stories to tell and many more the parents were never privy to for sure. One that comes to mind, and always brings a smile, is the time Andy and Mike decided to cruise the Las Vegas strip. Mike got Andy in his little car ... a feat in and of itself. So, without a wheelchair off they went. They decided they wanted to go to a number of casinos and thought renting a power chair was the answer. With ten dollars between them, they tried to rent a chair, only to find it cost considerably more for a mere hour or so. It appears the attendant was about their age and Mike convinced him to let them have a power chair for the whole evening for their $10, with the promise nothing would happen to it. So, off they went for hours of fun. Little did the attendant know that Mike had made a wheeled platform to stand on, while holding on to the power chair, so they could both "ride." A sight to behold, for sure, and a good time ensued.

Mike was a dear, special friend to Andy and we will always, always love him for that. To say he will be missed, just isn't enough. Not nearly enough. He touched his life in ways no one else could or would. Andy's life is so much better for having had Mike in it.

Lee and Marla Fair

Mikey & Andy High School Graduation

2006

"A lot of people have walked in and out of my life....but Mike was the only friend I wanted to be around forever. If it were not for him I would have taken my own life long ago."
Andy Fair

Andy wrote this in an email to me on January 21, 2015 ...

Dear Momma P:

I didn't have a lot of friends growing up, because I was born with Arthrogryposis, it's a form of MD. In short, I have a very limited range of motion and stiff joints. When I got to 7th grade, that all changed for me when I met Mike. Mike Portaro was one of the best people I have ever gotten the privilege to know. When we first met, I was in a very dark place in my life. My life was extremely difficult, physically and emotionally. Basically confined to a wheelchair, unless someone carries me to a chair, life just didn't make any sense. When I met Mike, I was 13, he saw that I could use a friend and that I probably could use someone to talk to. Indeed, I could and indeed I did. We quickly became the best of friends. He did so much for me. When I would randomly fall, I would call Mike to see if he would come pick me up off the floor. He would be there in a flash. I was very insecure around new people, but he didn't let that stop me. He quickly encouraged me that I have nothing to be afraid of and that people would love me for my great personality and big heart. To this very day, I live by what he said. I am no longer afraid to mingle with

16

new people, because of him and all the new friends I was able to make, is because of him. I am heartbroken and sad that he is no longer here, but I feel comforted in knowing that he will live on through me, because without him, I wouldn't be writing this today.

Love you,

Andrew L. Fair

This is one of many letters we received, that gave us a glimpse of what the world lost the day Mikey was shot to death, in the most brutal way, all for a car and his ticket money. It made the pain even worse to bare. Here we were grieving the life of our son. Someone with a good heart, the best heart. And, out there on the streets, somewhere, was his killer, still running loose. If his killer had just asked Mikey to get out of the car that night, if he had just told him what he wanted – knowing my son – he would have gladly given it all to him and probably included the shirt off his back.

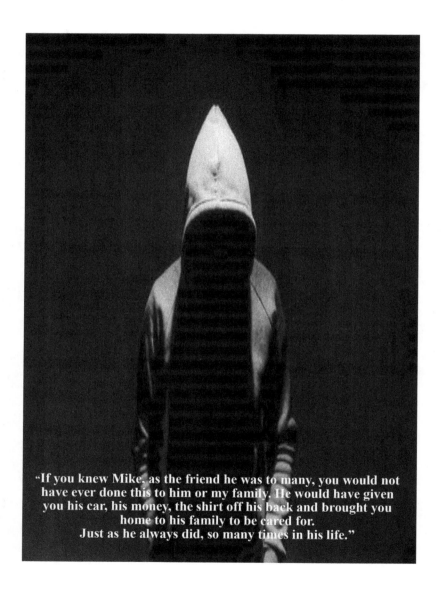

"If you knew Mike, as the friend he was to many, you would not have ever done this to him or my family. He would have given you his car, his money, the shirt off his back and brought you home to his family to be cared for.
Just as he always did, so many times in his life."

A Letter to My Son's Killer

I don't know what to say to you right now … I don't feel hate or want revenge against you. I ask the question over and over "why … my son!" Then, I am reminded that God gave His only Son so that we would have everlasting life! He did not give up his Son so that Jesus would be forgotten … but that the world would change. God only causes all things to work together for good to those who love God … to those who are called according to His purpose.

When Mikey was about seven years old … God spoke to me in prayer and told me "Do not worry about your son Michael, it is with him I have My greatest plans." Even though my heart is broken and grieving for my baby, this thought always made me smile … I must turn to the promise of God, that Mikey's life has a great purpose, it was predestined in *Romans 8:26–39.*

22 We know that the whole creation has been groaning as in the pains of childbirth right up to the present time. 23 Not only so, but we ourselves, who have the first fruits of the Spirit, groan inwardly as we wait eagerly for our adoption to sonship, the redemption of our bodies. 24 For in this hope we were saved. But hope that is seen is no hope at all. Who hopes for what they already have? 25 But, if we hope for what we do not yet have, we wait for it patiently.

26 In the same way, the Spirit helps us in our weakness. We do not know what we ought to pray for, but the Spirit himself intercedes for us through wordless groans. 27 And he who searches our hearts knows the mind of the Spirit, because the Spirit intercedes for God's people in accordance with the will of God.

19

28 And we know that in all things, God works for the good of those who love Him, who have been called according to His purpose. 29 For those God foreknew He also predestined to be conformed to the image of His Son, that he might be the firstborn among many brothers and sisters. 30 And those He predestined, He also called; those He called, He also justified; those He justified, He also glorified.

It will be the Word that I will stand on to honor his short life as Jesus' was here on earth. God is the one who will justify this loss for us all.

My hope for you is to know, I will be praying for you and those who surround you. Someone must have hurt you deeply, not having been born and raised to show compassion for another human life. Someone must have not loved you enough, so you could love people in return. I don't know you and you don't know me, but I know God and I know where you will be going. My God protects His people; "Vengeance is mine" says the Lord. I can't sit here and write this and pretend that I am not angry with you, you took my baby boy ... I can only trust in God that He will use this tragedy, as He used His own Son's tragedy.

Michael's life was short ... but fulfilled. If you knew him ... you would not have shot him for any apparent reason. He was loved and cared for, he was somebody's son, brother, grandson, cousin, nephew, friend. How can you disregard a life ... I don't understand how someone taught these principles to you? I'm sorry for you, if you were not somebody's baby boy.

I'm not sure where God will take us from here ... but, I do know that Mike will never be forgotten. God will take this tragedy and comfort our hearts. It is with great faith and belief God will use Mikey's life, even after his death, as He has used His own Son.

I want to say "I Love YOU" to Mike one more time. I want to tell him how so very proud I am of him ... one more time. I want him to make me laugh again and smile when I'm down ... one more time. I want to hold him and rub his head or give him a haircut. I want to make his favorite dinner and lunch ... or even preach and yell at him ... but, you took that away and maybe not today ... but, soon God will reveal you, so that one more mom, one more dad, one more sister, one more brother, one more grandparent, one more aunt, one more uncle, one more nephew, one more cousin, one more friend will not have to endure this pain that YOU caused my family.

God be with you ... young man ... I feel sorry for you when He gets a hold of you.

Mikey's Mom, Momma P

April 16, 2011

Two weeks after Mikey's death, I decided to tell his killer everything that he had taken from me and how devastated I felt about it. Not to his face, because he still had not been arrested yet for killing Mikey. But, I had to get it all off my chest, so when the police found him, he would know exactly what I thought about his decision to end Mikey's life.

The day we'd been waiting for, the arrest of Mikey's killer, didn't come for seven long weeks. It was a bittersweet day for my family. Yes, the killer was off the streets, unable to claim another victim, unable to hurt another family. However, the pain he'd caused our family was irreversible. Mikey was dead and this kid was alive and breathing. Waiting in a jail cell, innocent until proven guilty.

He heals the
wounds of
every
SHATTTERED
heart

Psalms 147:3

© Norina Leyde Photography

Chapter 4

A SHATTERED FAMILY

Parents are not the only family members, who experience deep grief and trauma, when one of their children dies. Siblings are traumatized differently than parents. They not only experience the loss of a brother or sister, they are now faced with the fact their parents are not the same people they once were. This is an entirely confusing and complicated grief to a child, no matter what age. Their family has been shattered and now, all of a sudden, it is never going to be the same. How can anyone expect a young life to handle this, when adults cannot even comprehend this life change?

After losing my older brother, Larry, when I was 23 years old, I'd like to say I understood how my children were feeling during the time following Mikey's death. However, losing my brother felt much different than losing my son. The emotions I had to see my family go through only added to the injustice of the situation and pain we all endured.

You never quite appreciate or understand the value of a life and their contributions, until you feel the void after the loss of their life. Our family certainly felt the void, and we all had our own ways of processing it.

Mikey was truly an encourager. He kept a list of positive quotes in his pocket he read every single day, before he left the house. I now have those tattered and tethered papers in a memory box. When our youngest son, Joey, was promoted to the varsity football team, as a freshman, in the 2008 season, he was somewhat intimidated at first. But, Mikey wasn't going to allow any of this in Joey's head. Mikey encouraged Joey he was good enough to play with the big boys. In the wristband quarterbacks wear to call plays, Mikey wrote this on the other side of them.

Joey (Lil Bro) Hey!

You're a superstar boy! Don't let anyone/anything tell you different! Know I'm always here watching you...always got your back kid...love ya...Mikey P

You have worked so hard and it has paid off! Don't let anyone steal your dream! Fight for what is yours!!! Never back down if you get knocked down get up!!! You are a legend bro!

"No dream is too small."
"No dream is too big."
"Whether you say you can or can't...you're right!"
"The hardest part of getting to the top of the ladder is getting through the crowd at the bottom!"

On June 4, 2011, at the East vs West State Conference game, Joey was voted Nevada State All Star. Just two months after Mikey's murder, Joey played his heart out, constantly looking up to the sky and opening that wristband reading **"I'm always here watching you...always got your back kid!"** What a beautiful treasure this will be passed down for many future generations. God knew Joey would need this one day... He never fails us...ever!!!

This was in the Las Vegas local newspaper the following day:

"Playing in an all-star game is memorable for any high school football player. Few will remember Saturday night's occasion like Faith Lutheran quarterback, Joe Portaro. Still coping with the tragic death of his older brother, Michael, Joe Portaro passed for 66 yards and a touchdown to lead the Sunset Region seniors to a 21-0 rout of the Sunrise in the 40th West Charleston Lions Club Charity All-Star Game at Bishop Gorman High School.

"Every time I wake up in the morning, I talk to Mike," Joe Portaro said. "Tonight, I went out and prayed. I dedicated this game to him."

Joe Portaro completed his first four passes and finished 5-for-9 on his way to overall Most Valuable Player honors. He fired a 7-yard TD strike to a Faith Lutheran teammate in the first quarter of the game."

While working on this book, I came across a letter that Mikey wrote about Joey:

What can I say about my little brother Joey! First off, he's basically my twin; we have a lot in common. I see my little brother and can smile, because of what he has achieved and what direction he is heading with his life. Joe is a leader in every aspect of life and he is never ashamed to be himself. On the football field, eyes are drawn to him and everyone looks to Joe as their captain and their leader. Off the field, all his friends follow in his footsteps, with everything he does. He's the life of the party and he knows that you don't have to be stupid to have fun.

Joey is one of the funniest dudes I have ever seen. At any given moment, he can make you laugh so hard, you almost cry. With just one look of his face, when he is trying to be funny, cracks me up because I know exactly what he is thinking, even without him speaking. Me and my brother can have the greatest time sitting in a room with nothing in it and laugh till we pass out.

Joey has a big heart and has a lot of love to offer people. I see it in the little things he does for people. He doesn't judge people the way that most kids do. He has the greatest spectrum of friends and I'm sure that everyone has nothing but great things to say about him. He isn't afraid to kick it with the nerd or the loser; because behind those broad shoulders, 6'4" frame and pretty smile, he is one. He's as goofy as anyone could ever be and people love it and I'm so happy he isn't ashamed of it.

I don't have anything to say about my little brother, other than the fact that when he farts it smells like the backyard of a sewage dump. Other than that, all I have to say about my little brother is that not only is he my brother, but he is my best friend and I could not ask for anyone better to fill his place. I Love You Bro!!!

Mikey P

Mikey's death was incredibly shocking for all of us, but for my youngest daughter, Chrissy, it seemed to be the most difficult. Since the day Chrissy was born, she and Mikey had an out-of-the ordinary link. He was seven years old when she was born. I had never heard of a child this age being thrilled to feed or change a baby's diaper. But Mikey would stay inside and help me with her, while his brothers would be playing in the backyard or swimming in the pool. I can still see the smile on his face, as he would look at me with amazement over her dainty body. It was because of Mikey that she got her nickname, Peanut.

From that time forward, they grew into this protective force that no one would ever be able to penetrate. In their teens, they spent countless hours taking pictures, making videos and dancing to music as "Papa Americano". Thankfully, we have several of these great, fun memories to watch and treasure.

When Chrissy was in fourth grade, she took up volleyball and Mikey never missed her games, unless he was working. She seemed to learn the art of hitting the ball harder, during the time after his death, than anyone could ever imagine. Chrissy's coaches loved having her as "middle", since she and her 5'10" tall, thin frame could jump three to four feet off the court and hit the ball so hard, aiming at times for her opponent's head. At one game, she hit this poor girl in the head so hard, it knocked her head back and almost put her flat on the court. The playback video was posted on Facebook, as the hit of the week, by her coach.

Although all of our family was deeply affected by Mikey's death, the loss was particularly devastating to Chrissy. The pain and trauma of Mikey's death was extremely difficult for Chrissy, and the emotions for my family were more than unbearable when reality kicked in for us all. Volleyball was Chrissy's public outlet to vent most of her pain. But, at home, her pain came out in angry tears, sobbing and literally yelling, "I just want to go be with Mikey."

Counseling did not seem to help the nightmares Chrissy experienced in the middle of the night, sobbing, "I want Mikey!"

All I could do, as a mother, was to hold Chrissy and cry with her, understanding the depth of her pain. Near the end of the summer, when school started, and volleyball games began, we had found a counselor for Chrissy individually, who seemed to be finally helping her to understand her emotional trauma. We felt encouraged she would survive this nightmare. However, bursts of anger still came out at home from all of us and especially in a 16-year-old full of teen hormones. I knew Chrissy was strong, and stubborn and would not allow this devastation and loss to totally conquer her future successes. I prayed she would use this loss in our lives to show others how God can heal the broken.

If you aren't going all the way...why go at all.

If you aren't going all the way...why go at all.

If you aren't going all the way...why go at all.

Victory belongs to the most persevering

Dreams....are the touchstones of our character.

The only job you start at the top is digging the hole!!!

MEMORY...
IS THE SCRIBE OF THE
SOUL

The toughest part of getting to the top of the ladder is getting through the crowd at the bottom.

No Pain...No Gain

NEVER SAY DIE

You can be they if they think... "You Can"

Dream / Strength

"You are never a loser until You stop trying"

Nothing succeeds like success

NEVER SAY DIE

"If you can't accept loosing... You Can't Win"

It takes a great deal of courage to stand up to enemies...but even more to stand up to your friends.

To win without risk is to triumph without

Confidence is the hinge on the door to success!

If at first you don't succeed...try...try again

A man fall in love through his eyes...a woman through her ears

No dreamer is ever too small, no dream is too big

You are never a Loser Until You Stop Trying

Skill and Confidence are an Unconquerable Army

Success only hurts the first time

Happiness depends on ourselves... and God

"In life, we loved you dearly; in death we love you still. In our hearts you hold a place no one else will ever fill."

Chapter 5

THE UNTHINKABLE

"Nobody can go back and start a new beginning...but, anyone can start today and make a new ending."

On Mother's Day 2011, only a short time after Mikey's death, our 16-year old daughter, Chrissy, wrote this quote on a card she had given to me. These words gave me hope she would be okay and will be able to move forward with her young life, despite the pain she was experiencing.

It was difficult for everyone in our family. But, life's routines had to resume. Joey and Chrissy were out of school for at least a month, maybe a month and a half after Mikey's death. I was out of work about the same amount of time. Having to return to work proved to be an even more difficult task than I had expected, since Mikey and I worked together. We worked at a lot of the casinos and, for the work we did, had to sign in with various securities. One of the first days back to work, I walked up to the sign-in sheet, saw Mikey's signature, felt like I was going to throw up, and immediately turned around to leave. The reality he would no longer be signing in to work with me made it so real he was gone and unfortunately for everyone ... forever.

Chrissy went back to volleyball practice. Being around her teammates seemed to help. Joey was graduating from high school in June. His mind was focused on graduation and college plans. Rico moved into his own apartment, because he felt being in our house, with pictures of Mikey, was too difficult for him.

As Labor Day Weekend was approaching and volleyball had a break from its hectic schedule, Chrissy asked me if I would take her and a girlfriend, Chandler, up to our mountain condo, located in Brian Head, Utah. I thought it would be a great idea to get away to the place she loved so dearly. We felt the surroundings were so close to God; a place of peace created by "The Almighty". Whether it was winter snowboarding or hiking and riding ATV'S during the summer, it was our place to be together, away from the hustle and bustle of everyday struggles.

We unloaded the car and headed to our friend's place. The summer weather was perfect – cool and sunny. It was Saturday, September 3, 2011, many families were barbequing while others were out riding horses, ATV's, and bicycles. Chrissy prepared herself and her friend for an exploratory tour of the mountain trails on the ATVs. There was an abandoned old school bus she loved going to see, where they would take hundreds of pictures. What young 16-year-old girl doesn't take too many pictures?

I stayed back with my friends for a visit and to watch Chrissy's last volleyball tournament, where she had knocked the girl so hard in the head. Seriously, what parent doesn't like to brag about their kid's athletic ability? At 6:15 p.m., my phone rang. It was Chrissy calling me.

"Hi honey, I was just showing everyone your video."

A man's voice startled me, "You better get up here right away, there's been an accident!"

"What?" My heart raced as the words settled in my mind. *An accident?* "Where? Where are you? Where's my daughter?"

"Aspen Road, it's serious."

"Chrissy's been in an accident." I shouted out, grabbed my keys, and ran out the door. My heart was pounding out of my chest, as I drove out of there like a "bat out of hell". Talking aloud to my friend Berta, "What if she broke her leg? She won't be able to play volleyball."

"What is this going to do to her, with all the devastation we've been dealing with?"

"She probably broke her arm or something."

"But he said serious. How serious is serious?"

The five-minute drive up the road, we had driven for so many years, seemed like hours. My heart pounded, and my anxiety heightened, as I pulled up to the accident scene, looking at what seemed like something out of a crime scene of spectators. There was Chrissy, her lifeless body lying limp on the side of the road. "Why aren't any of these people with her? Why is she lying there all alone?" My friends MJ, Jackie, and Desiree followed quickly behind, up the mountain.

As I ran over to her, I knew immediately, she was already dead. "Dead, how can this be?" Chrissy's body was cold and lifeless; there was no movement. I screamed for a blanket, "She's cold, get me a blanket!" I lied down next to my girl on the cold gravel road. Stroking her blood drenched hair and caressing her ice-cold face, as blood oozed out of her ears and mouth. "My baby! My baby!

34

"This is impossible." I yelled, "We just lost Mikey; I can't live without you, too."

It seemed as if I were in a movie, filled with horror, having an out-of-body experience. My heart lost life, lying there holding her. Wounds so deep, you don't even want to have a heart to feel the brutal pain. "It's not fair. Why?" I cried, "Why this again?"

How could she have been crushed by a machine she loved to ride so much. She was a "badass" on these machines since she was four years old. I could hear Chandler, her friend, screaming, traumatized by what she'd witnessed. Her screams seemed so distant, even though she was standing near. I could not move, I could not leave her, not my baby girl. Someone tried to pull me off Chrissy, but I screamed, "I will not leave. I want to go with her, someone please just shoot me!"

My friend, Rick, a 6'5" strong, gentle giant, who absolutely loved my daughter, tried to pull me away from Chrissy's body quietly, explaining to me, "Cynthia, the paramedics and police need to do their job."

"Their job?" I wailed, "What job? She's not a job," I fought to get back to her body, "she's my baby!"

There in the middle of the road, being held back by Rick, I began taking my anguish up with God. "What the f---, God! What did I do to deserve this again?" I screamed, as I watched the paramedics attend to my daughter's body, "How could you do this to us...again?"

"Someone, please, kill me, please, kill me now! I can't do this again!" I screamed over and over. Losing Mikey was devastating enough. It was an unbearable pain I was working

35

through day-by-day. Seeing Chrissy's body lying lifeless on that road unraveled everything I was working through.

At some point, I fought a police officer in the middle of the road and tried to grab his gun to shoot myself. It was then they had to physically secure me and put me into the backseat of my Navigator. Rick drove me to his place, while his wife, Desiree, and our friend, Mark, stayed with Chrissy's body until she was taken to the city morgue. I cried on the bedroom floor, for what seemed like hours, repeating the words, "I want to die! I just want to die." No one knew what to do with me.

My friends there with me had just experienced the murder of my son, Mikey, just five months ago and now this. How could this be true? The words "in shock" took on an entire new meaning for all of us ... especially me after witnessing what just happened.

I called my mother and my friend, Pastor Denise, screaming out to them, "Christina's dead, Christina's dead!"

They both told me they could not understand what I was saying through the sobs and screams. All they could say was, "What? What are you saying?"

My mother kept repeating, "Cynthia, don't you mean Michael?"

I can feel the pain and anxiety of that outcry, while I write this, through my flood of tears, with what remains all these years later, a broken heart.

I don't remember how I returned to my own bed and condo. I stayed there, drugged on something for over three days, with Chrissy's pillow over my head, sobbing out to God.

The scent of her pillow was overwhelmingly alive to me ... as I buried my face in it. The images of my baby on that cold gravel road plummeted through my mind, playing repeatedly on rewind mode. I thought of the many times we had lied in this bed, cuddling and watching old movies or doing homework, after a long hike in the woods. She loved to play games, Catch Phrase, Gestures, Yahtzee and cards were among all our family favorites. It seemed the place she loved would no longer be in my life. How could I come back here again, to relive this, and relive the loss of my baby girl or sleep in this bed, where we slept, since Chrissy was a little girl, with her beautiful petite hands I'd loved to hold? We shared so many amazing memories, in this little condo, in this comfy bed. "How can I live without her and Mikey too? How will I live ... again?"

My husband, Richard, came into the bedroom after lying there for three days, and said to me, "It's time to go home."

Richard asked me, the night before her memorial, if I wanted to speak at the service, and I said, "How can we do this again?" And, before he could say a word, I abruptly answered, "NO WAY!"

In the morning, lying in bed, with my head buried under her pillow. The Lord clearly spoke to me, as if He were in the room, and said, "I gave you them!"

"Them?" I thought bewildered, "Who are them?"

Then all of these familiar faces and names started coming to my mind, first my family, then close friends, then the volleyball team, people who have been family to us since we moved to Las Vegas in 1984 and... those incredible people from Chrissy's school, Faith Lutheran. He asked me to share this at her memorial to offer hope and trust in Him. I'm still not sure how He gave me the strength to do this, but I was obedient to His request. I began to write out names of people and families, who had been there for us, not only throughout life, but especially since Mikey's death.

There were about 1,200 people at Chrissy's memorial service and about 600 or more watching online. Unbelievably, the same as Mikey's. First, I said, despite my outburst on the road, I was not angry with God. Then I shared what The Lord had spoken to me that morning and asked each person, family or teams to stand, as I called their names, in the sanctuary. I personally thanked each person or group for the sacrifices and love poured out from everyone, who were present, on our behalf. At the end of speaking, every person in the sanctuary was standing. I closed with, "And this is how we will do this. Together we can do all things through Christ who strengthens us!"

It took me an entire year, after Chrissy's death, to return to Brian Head. I needed to go to the place where I had last held my baby. It was on September 3, 2012, the one-year anniversary of her death. I sat in my car alone on the side of the road, sobbing for hours, thinking of that horrific day. Finally, coming to a place in my heart, I felt like I needed to ask God to forgive me for screaming and yelling at Him, using the kind of profanity I did. There had to be reconciliation with Him, for my grieving soul, to find healing.

"We are therefore Christ's ambassadors, as though God were making his appeal through us. We implore you on Christ's behalf: Be reconciled to God". 2 Corinthians 5:20 NIV

Reacting the way I did made me think, I didn't show a good example of being a very Christian-like woman. Since then,

I have asked those who were there that day for forgiveness. Of course, everyone said they would have done the same or worse and couldn't believe how I have handled both of my children's deaths. Being an example of Christ was important to me for my mourning family and I did not want anyone to fear I would take my own life.

To lose two children so brutally and tragically within five months of each other is the ultimate shock in the oceans of life's suffering. Living through the violent death of a child, who was so loved and cared for, is an unthinkable act of humanity. Then, to lose another in such a horrible accident ... it's difficult to put into words. In case those thoughts just ran through your mind, "This hasn't happened to me or won't happen to me." Well, contrary to most people's beliefs, it does happen and to many of us. If you are one of the fortunate to go through life without blemish ... praise God for it, every single day.

Brian Head is not the same for our family and me. We don't go nearly as often as we did over the past 20-plus years. However, I am so very grateful for being blessed to share so many incredible family and friend's memories in our little place we call home.

I later learned from a note left on the cross from people we did not know, the cross-handmade by a very kind man, Mike, to place at the scene of the accident. A woman, who apparently thought Chrissy was her granddaughter, started administering CPR to her. This is the note little 13-year old Jordan left on the cross ...

"I am so very sorry for your loss. I remember arriving on my four-wheeler and wondered what was going on. When I realized my heart sank. My grandmother had given her CPR trying to revive her. My grandma thought your daughter was me, because we look similar. I can't imagine the pain you must be in! If I could have traded in your daughter's place, I would have in a heartbeat! You will always be in our prayers. Love Jordan Marie Jacobson (age 13)"

Several other notes were placed on the cross in a Ziploc bag from the people standing in the road who personally witnessed Chrissy's accident, as I pulled up to this horrific scene. Notes of prayers and so much love poured out for our family ... I can only thank them through my own personal prayers of gratitude for trying to save my baby girl's life.

Today, because of two very special people, one being my Mom, the other an old friend, as a birthday gift, I now own the property where Chrissy's accident happened on Aspen Road. My dream is that one day, I will be able to afford to develop it in a beautiful way to honor my children.

It is important to remind ourselves how precious life really is, and it does go on, only so much more differently. When I think about all of this now, my heart smiles with the love shown to my family, because Chrissy and Mikey continue to live in those who knew them. We visit the property regularly and surround ourselves with memories we will cherish for generations to come.

One day, I believe and declare, God will speak to me in His timing and show me just how much He will do with this pain. I keep asking Him.

"It's been nine years *God*, Hello."

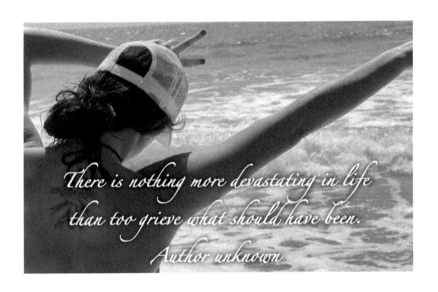

There is nothing more devastating in life
than too grieve what should have been.
Author unknown

Chapter 6

Christina Nicole Portaro

"Chrissy P"
(April 26, 1995 – September 3, 2011)

"Life is Not Measured by the Number of Breaths we Take, But by the Moments That Take Our Breath Away."- author unknown

My beautiful daughter, Chrissy, had the ability to take your breath away by the laughter she would bring into any setting or conversation. She lived "larger" than life for most of her short 16½ years. This speaks volumes, when more than 1,200 people, not including online viewers, attended her Celebration of Life Memorial. It was just a glimpse of how many people she touched and how much joy she would bring to those who were fortunate enough to be part of her life. Chrissy's first love was her family and close friends. As I look at the hundreds of photos taken of her over the years, it was obvious ... she surely enjoyed life to the max.

Chrissy loved dressing up for any occasion. She loved doing her make-up, her hair and picking out the perfect outfit ... whether for a school dance, school spirit day, a party, any holiday and, of course, Halloween. If there was a function ... she knew exactly what she would wear from top to bottom. It was my absolute joy to shop during a mother/daughter spree. I especially miss those times shopping together. Growing up, one of her favorite playtime activities was to go into Mommy's closet or jewelry box and play dress up. From the featured photos, she was quite the "Princess P", as I would often call her by her nickname, which was "Peanut".

The picture above was taken shortly after her older brother, Mikey, was killed on March 30, 2011. She literally pushed herself through the pain of loss to move forward and enjoy what was to be her first and only prom, her sophomore year of high school. Just five months later, a few weeks into her junior year ... her young, big, beautiful life ended tragically and quickly in the ATV accident.

There wasn't much Chrissy did not love or love to do. She was an MVP Volleyball player, receiving letters from colleges around the country to recruit her during her sophomore year. The letters continued to pour in for years after her death. She was an advocate for the underdog and despised bullying. She would stick up for everyone, who was teased, or picked on at school ... she was full of expression of her beliefs ... positive or negative. I received a phone call in the middle of the day from her counselor that I needed to come to school, because

Chrissy was in trouble. When I arrived, Chrissy was sitting in the counselor's office with her very sarcastic and annoyed look on her face. The first thing I asked was, "What happened?"

The counselor said that Chrissy had used the "F" word. I was pretty stunned, but not surprised, because she does have three older brothers, who are all athletes. I asked Chrissy why she would use such a word, "Hello, you go to a Christian school?"

Her answer, "Mom, this jerk made fun of my friend, Clayton." Clayton was, at the time, a student in the school's Mark 10:14 Program for special needs students, where Chrissy volunteered. She continued, "I told him to shut his "F'N" mouth, pushed him against the wall, and told him to never treat anyone like he just did."

My response to that was easy, "So, what is the problem here and is the boy in trouble? Were his parents called to school?"

The Counselor, in a round-about way, said there wasn't anything that would be done with the boy. However, because Chrissy swore, she needed to go home for the day.

I replied, "I am so proud of you for sticking up for Clayton. Let's go Christina, we're going shopping."

Just like her brother, Mikey, Chrissy had a huge heart for the underdogs. After her death, I received a card from the students of the Mark 10:14 Program. Here's what they had to say...

"Christina was so kind to our students in the Mark 10:14 Program; she often sat with Billy at lunch and was willing to speak up when she saw other students being

unkind to him. Her compassion and integrity were a gift to us. We will miss her. My prayers are with you in this hard, hard time." Mrs. Lee

"I am sorry. I miss her. She is my friend all the time." Clayton

"I am sorry for my heart to break. I love Chrissy P." Billy

"I am sorry you have to be sad." Bailey

"There are no words to describe this loss. I hope you get some really good comfort and I am praying for you." Jasmine

"I love you, Cynthia." Alyssa

"She will always be in our hearts. She was very nice to me." Julia

"I am sad, very sad!" Austin

———

"The people brought children to Jesus, hoping he might touch them. The disciples shooed them off. But Jesus was irate and let them know it: "Don't push these children away. Don't ever get between them and me. These children are at the very center of life in the kingdom. Mark this: Unless you accept God's kingdom in the simplicity of a child, you'll never get in." Then, gathering the children up in his arms, he laid his hands of blessing on them. Mark 10:14-16 MSG

———

Chrissy served on numerous committees, volunteering with younger kids, no matter what their capacity. She loved coaching volleyball, during the summer breaks, with the younger players. She would come home sharing stories with me, making me laugh at how cute these little girls were. I will never forget her laugh and still hear it in my soul just about every day.

Her zest for life was uncontainable. She could tell a story and bring it to life as if you were present in it. Serving others was one of my favorite gifts she possessed ... she wore her heart on her sleeves and gave it to others freely. Serving the homeless, donating socks, gloves, blankets, food and other miscellaneous items was one of her favorite things to do. She had no fear of sharing stories with the homeless, making them laugh while giving them a cup of coffee or hot chocolate and offering one of her special bear hugs. She truly lived with the heart and soul of Christ; who she is named after.

Our Church Youth Pastor, Derek Bareman, spoke at Chrissy's memorial and said, "Chrissy was the zest of our youth group. She loved big and she loved Christ so much that she is the only 16-year-old, who was baptized, more than anyone in their entire lifetime. I had to tell her on our last retreat to San Diego, "Chrissy, you don't have to be baptized every time we have a baptism." "She gave me that look of hers and said, "Oh yes I do ... it always makes me feel so new and ready to give all my sin back to God." Chrissy was baptized many times; first as a baby, then when she was eight years old at church, twice in California oceans, at 12-years-old, in a friend's backyard Jacuzzi by Pastor Jimmy Coyle, and once in the Atlantic Ocean, by her Uncle Richard and Aunt Theresa. I'm pretty sure she was covered.

This was written in a card from one of her favorite teachers ... **Dear Portaro Family: "Words cannot express what I am feeling; in my state, I still can't imagine the pain that exists in your hearts. Please know – Christina was my joy, my pleasure, and my pride at Faith Lutheran! Not only did I see her in American Literature, but she was my aide this year. M-1 gets pretty lonely for me. I miss Christina's smile, her enthusiasm, and the stories she loved to tell about her family. She really loved people; that love still shines in my classroom and my heart. Christina has taken a piece of my heart with her. I look forward to the day I am allowed to see her in Heaven. Thank you for sharing your beautiful daughter with the world. She left us way too soon. With love and sympathy." Kim Thiel**

I was listening to Chrissy talking to a friend when she was about four years old. Our favorite mailman, Rodney, came to the door. He had a package for her from my friend, Theresa, her Godmother. After opening it, Chrissy began to explain to her little friend how she had her very own "Fairy Godmother!" From that moment on, Theresa was just that to her.

This was written in a card from her Fairy Godmother, Aunt Theresa ... **"Cynthia, thank you for honoring me with the blessing of being Christina's, Godmother. In fact, "Fairy Godmother!" She will always have an impact on our lives, every day we breathe. Her presence filled us with so much love and joy. Know we love you and will continue to be your strength in this time of such great loss." Love you forever and always little Sissy, Richard and Theresa Ann Marie.**

Here are just a few more encouraging words I received after her death.

"Chrissy, you were an amazing person and friend to everyone. You'll live in my heart forever, and I will really miss you. You're the person I always strived to be." Love Jordyn

"I really love The Portaro's. Christina was my role model!" Love Anabelle

"R.I.P. Christina, everyone will miss you and your contagious laugh." Love Lexi

"I will miss seeing Christina every day after school, in the gym, getting ready for practice. It was my personal duty to find something to tease her about, just so I could see that smile!" Coach Bret Walter

"A favorite memory of Christina is sitting on the bench last season and her hugging my son, Jett, after every match. I will miss her so much." Coach Sharia Washington

I wish you could have known my daughter Chrissy, as many do ... there is not much you would not have loved about her. She was known as "Feisty Momma" by her peers at school, and she was admired for her leadership and passion for people. Even in all the girl drama ... LOL ... If you have teen daughters, you understand and get what I mean.

Fortunately for us, Chrissy loved filming videos with her brothers and many of her BFFs. It is very valuable to have those memories now and to be able to look at some of those and hear her voice, with that crazy laugh of hers. Chrissy also knew how I loved to journal. She would write little love notes in them and would kiss several pages with my pink lipstick. I have one on my closet door that I found shortly after her death. She drew a picture of me, holding her hands, with

"SHOPPING" in quotes. I sure miss her presence ... we were close and enjoyed being together.

Yes, we did have an occasional argument that never lasted very long. More so, after Mikey died, she was extremely vocal and angry. I could hear Chrissy sobbing in her room for hours, calling out to Mikey. I would simply hold her fetal position, and cry with her, while she would quietly say, "I wanna go be with Mikey, Mom." How do you console a child in their pain? Other than just listen and hold them, while you both cry, experiencing the pain together.

I could go on forever about her. She was a mini-me, people would say. I think you can see, after reading about her young life, Chrissy was a light in the dark clouds of life. I am very thankful to all who loved her and so deeply.

It has been written, "A child is to have your heart forever, walking outside your body." That forever does not change, just because they are not here in our presence. The heart will, always and forever, treasure them as children we have given birth to. Children are a gift from God. Please treasure the memories and always speak words of life into their souls. They, after all, are extremely valuable to your existence.

A LETTER TO MY DAUGHTER

It's so difficult to believe that you aren't here with us ... gone way too soon ... "they say." Your life touched mine so deeply, it's difficult for me to describe just how much. I guess it took losing you to understand just how much you meant to me and how deeply we do love our children. As I look at the memories we made together and how proud I am of you ... and that God gave me you to hold close within my heart and soul ... if only for a little while. As I look at the pictures of your birth to the pictures last taken of you ... It sinks into my heart of tears, there will be no more memories to share with you, no pictures, no proms, no birthdays, a wedding or children, and the joy of your laughter for the rest of my lifetime.

How sad that families have to go through losing a child to a senseless accident, murder, sickness, suicide or an act of terrorism ... even an act of God. "Why?" I ask. Why? Not my child .... Don't take my child. Is that selfish? Why not mine? Who am I? I'm really not that special. Why someone else's kid and not mine? I never had any of these thoughts until losing Mikey and now you. Hey, tell God we gave Him two ... does that not mean anything? It's sad being part of this club ... I despise the pain we all have to endure. There is nothing normal about this and there will never be a "new normal" for me ... ever. Not without my children here with their family who misses and loves them so dearly. It's a jail sentence for me.

These are just a few things that riddle through my brain almost every day we have to be without you. Through these tough times, I have found some peace through God's grace.

He touches my heart somehow that soothes my soul and spirit. His touch is gentle, kind and patient ... as He tells us to be in 1 Corinthians 13:4 ... Love is patient, Love is kind. It does not envy, it does not boast, it is not proud.

I sat on that cold dirt road holding your lifeless body, broken but so angelic. I collapsed in tears and shock knowing you were gone from us, but not your soul and spirit. I loved you even more at that moment and always forever.

Dear Christina, if you are reading this ... I love you the most right now.

Happy Birthday Peanut ... Mom

April 26, 2012

SHE STOOD IN THE STORM & WHEN THE WIND DID NOT BLOW HER WAY, SHE ADJUSTED HER SAILS.

Chapter 7

ARE YOU KIDDING ME!

"Now faith is confidence in what we hope for and assurance about what we do not see." Hebrews 11:1

So ... I'm sure your head is spinning, with the life-changing events I've shared with you. I know I've had to take a few breaks and grab a whole lotta tissue, while reliving these experiences, as I wrote them down. First, Mikey, then Chrissy. Life was truly flipped upside down for my family. Somehow, only by the grace of God, we managed to get through the holidays and continue going on with everyday life, each day, but certainly not ordinary for us. There were two, deep, empty holes in our family and on top of everything, the courts still hadn't closed Mikey's case. The defense attorney submitted multiple appeals regarding the case, to delay the trial.

It was April 2012, and although a little over a year had passed since Mikey's murder, his killer still sat in a jail cell, unsentenced. My husband attended all the postponements at the courthouse. I was still perfectly fine, never having to lay eyes on Brandon J. Hill.

Around that time, I was asked to speak at Faith's high school chapel. It's kind of similar to an assembly in public schools, but they have worship and then a guest speaker. Our family was very connected with Faith Lutheran – Rico, Mikey, and Joey had all graduated from there. So, it was no surprise when the principal called me to speak on faith. What was a surprise, though, was the date the principal chose, April 26 –

Chrissy's birthday! When I asked the principal, what made him choose that day, he answered, "Just random, would you like to change it?"

It may have been random, in his mind, but I believed God had to be up to something really good. The same week, three days before speaking, I had a routine colonoscopy scheduled. Who, in their right mind, schedules a colonoscopy the same week of a speaking engagement? Yep, me! Little did I know at the time I was about to face yet another wave of destruction.

I woke up from the colonoscopy with the doctor shaking me. He informed me he'd found a very large tumor in my colon, and I needed to return to his office later in the day for the results. My friend, Mary Jo, had driven me to the medical center for the procedure. When I asked if she would take me back that afternoon, I felt obligated to let her know why.

Her mouth dropped when I told her and she said, "What, what did you just say? Are you kiddin' me?" She's from Alabama, so imagine it said with a loud, strong, southern drawl. Mary Jo had been there devotedly through the loss of both children. The afternoon drive to the doctor's office had us both in a state of shock, asking, "God, are you kidding me?" Over, and over, again, and again.

When we arrived at his office, the doctor was on the phone talking to someone and it was about me. I wasn't very thrilled he was discussing my case in his office hallway for all to hear. It didn't put me in the best mood for the upcoming appointment, which went like this...

"You have a very large tumor in your Descending Colon." The doctor started off saying, "You need to make an appointment and see this group of doctors (he rattled off the names, of course) who handle these types of tumors, immediately. I believe, because of its size, it has to be cancerous. I have already sent your paperwork, and a sample, to the lab, for a biopsy. It is my opinion that you should get your affairs in order, because you most likely only have six months to live."

My heart began to beat to a different drummer, at what I would call, several pounding beats per second. My spirit woman arose, as I jumped off the table, wanting to hit something and I boldly said back to him, "Listen, Doc, you don't know who you are talking to or "Whose" you are talking too. You may be a doctor, but my "Physician" above is the only One that will put a number on my days. *You* are not Him!"

I looked at Mary Jo and we rushed out of the office, both of us in pissed-off mode, with this scripture running through my veins.

"My frame was not hidden from you when I was made in the secret place, when I was woven together in the depths of the earth. 16 Your eyes saw my unformed body; all the days ordained for me were written in your book before one of them came to be. 17 How precious to me are your thoughts, God! How vast is the sum of them! 18 Were I to count them, they would outnumber the grains of sand— when I awake, I am still with you." Psalm 139:15–18

I believed, for the first time in my life, questioning God and His plans for it, were more than justified. I had many questions I wanted Him to answer. *Ya think?*

"Why me?" "What did I do to deserve this now?" "Why my family?"

Needless to say, the biggest question I faced that day was, "How do I tell this to my children? After losing two of the most important people in their lives ... now their Mom is faced with a life-threatening disease?"

We decided to spare our three remaining children from any heartache until we had further details. I told my husband and my Mother, and of course, Mary Jo knew. I may have jumped off the table and proclaimed who my God is to the doctor, but I simply cannot describe the lack of faith I felt that day. Did I really want to be here? I was so drained from crying for my children in heaven, now I was crying for my living children. How would we all survive this?

On top of the sucker-punch news delivered at the appointment, I needed to decide if I had the strength to speak to the high school students, just ahead, in two days. Once again, empowered by a strength beyond what I could muster up on my own, I chose to keep the speaking arrangement at the school.

I decided to speak about the ability we all have to proclaim our destinies in Christ Jesus. Little did everyone in the room know, I was taking in every word for myself, as it left my mouth. "Each and every one of you, sitting in this room, has a purpose. It is something Chrissy would want for every single young adult, listening to this message."

I spoke about Chrissy's love for people and asked them to value the life they have been given and to honor each other and never speak disrespectfully to another or, especially, never bully anyone! Nobody deserves to be mistreated. This was my message to them.

After speaking, I said, "This is how we will honor your fallen classmate, who lived life this way. Make a friend with an underdog. Make a friend with someone less confident than you. Your compassion and friendship could help build their self-esteem." I handed out wristbands that said: *BE A SOMEBODY, TO SOMEBODY.*

A young girl came up to me after chapel and told me she had it all planned out, how she was going home to take her life that same day. But, she changed her mind, because of the words I had spoken. I think, making the decision to speak was a valuable one. Both Mikey and Chrissy had a huge passion for befriending underdogs. All my kids are like that! In fact, it was after a classmate of Joey's committed suicide, I decided to start the Facebook page, "No Buddy". The purpose of the page is to bring light to the epidemic of abuse, needing to change for our youth.

After recognizing the fact, we are now in this battle of cancer, my husband, Richard, and I began exploring options for my treatment. We made the decision to see a doctor at UCLA Medical Center. One of the top physicians in the country took my case immediately. What a blessing that was to us! The doctor reviewed my scans and said my chances of overcoming this were high, but the battle was going to be a long one and not very easy. I would need surgery to remove the large tumor and endure the possibility of chemotherapy.

I let out a short sigh of relief as I thought, "*OMG ... Thank You, Lord.*" Those words spoken gave us the hope God was in fact, in control and no one had the right to alter, or predict, our destinies. "*I will live!*"

Since we had all the facts, we decided to tell our boys, Rico and Joey, at a vacation spot in Southern California. I took a long walk with Joey, first explaining everything to him, with very encouraging words, that I will beat this. Well, I realized it didn't do very much good, as he fell to the ground and yelled up to God, "Don't you dare take my Mother from me! I can't live without her. I will kill myself, if she dies!"

His displays of emotions were accompanied by many cuss words. His anger was extremely painful to witness, knowing how difficult it was for him, already fighting to overcome the death of his siblings, just eight months before.

Rico, on the other hand, took the news quietly and reserved. This has always been his personality. So many times, over the years, I have worried about him, *because* he can withdraw his emotions quickly. However, this time was a little different. His eyes filled with tears and the tense look on his face got tighter; I knew the news deeply hurt him. He only spoke these words to me... "Momma, if anyone can kick this thing, it would be you."

I knew I had to be strong, for however my sons might take this news. When Rico told me those words, I believed him. And, at that moment, something arose in me, to fight for my life, like the lioness I am.

Our oldest, Maressa, lives in Washington State, so we had to share the news with her over the phone. She reacted the same as the boys, encouraging me to win, but with a heavy heart.

Surgery was scheduled for late May of 2012 ... it was all the doctor had available. Here I was, diagnosed with colon cancer right around Chrissy's birthday and going into surgery right around Mikey's birthday. Some might see these as purely coincidental, but I saw them as God perfectly setting things up.

After surgery, and a few days of recovery, Richard was so sweet to wheel me down to the Garden of Prayer. There, I was surprised by family members holding baby blue balloons, to release, in honor of Mikey's birthday. I could really feel the presence of God in that garden. There was an undeniable peace. He has been with us all along and was not going to allow the enemy to take me down or out.

I won't go into much detail about the battle of chemotherapy, and the effects I lived through for the six months following the surgery. If you have personally gone through this disease, or witnessed a loved one, you know it's not a happy journey.

In July, just two months into this journey, I received a phone call, asking me if I would consider moving, part-time to Camarillo, CA, to be their Project Manager and Designer for a very prestigious 45,000-square-foot AeroSpace facility renovation. All my living and traveling expenses would be covered, but the project would take at least a year to complete. Oh boy, what didn't fly through my brain? How would I survive doing this job, while undergoing intense chemotherapy? The CEO agreed that taking care of myself should be a top priority during the project and I could work three weeks and take a week off to head home.

The week off wouldn't be any kind of vacation or break. During those weeks, I would drive home to Las Vegas and receive the intravenous chemotherapy. I'd sit for hours receiving this treatment through a port that had been implanted in my chest. The additional three weeks, I'd return to the worksite, where I'd continue the treatment in pill form, which made me violently ill. The general contractors and I would be in a meeting, and I'd have to excuse myself to go throw-up. Not the most enjoyable season of my life. However, I did the job. It's amazing how we can push through these trials! My daily mantra was, "You Just Gotta Have Faith!"

Only a select few at the facility actually knew what I was going through at the time. Funny how my lack of hair didn't give anyone a clue. Some people hear my story and think I'm a strong woman, but I attribute my strength entirely to God. God will give us His strength to endure life's greatest battles, with victories on the horizon. Learning to turn every doubt, or any fears, over to Him, is truly a battlefield of the mind. This life surely will test your Faith, Hope and Trust, for His plans to redeem, when the enemy tries to defeat us.

"No weapon forged against you will prevail, and you will refute every tongue that accuses you. This is the heritage of the servants of the Lord, and this is their vindication from me, declares the Lord." Isaiah 54:17 (NIV)

I have always believed standing on scripture is a necessity for our lives, if we want to live as overcomers.

"I can do ALL things through Christ, who strengthens me, (Philippians 4:13)" is one of my favorite self-talks, accompanied with a lot of deep, heavy breathing.

I'll take a moment to add that the building renovation turned out to be amazing, thanks to several perfect team members, who had my back during the entire project. However, ... in the midst of the project, another wave was on the horizon.

Now, I had to put my faith into what I was about to hear.

In October, of the same year, 2012, Richard informed me he had been diagnosed with Squamous Cell Carcinoma. It is the most common type of nasal cavity and Para nasal Sinus Cancer.

OMG ...*"Are you kidding me!"*

For the next two years, Richard battled as best anyone could, with such a horrific cancer. In those two years, he endured two very invasive surgeries and two six-month rounds of chemotherapy and radiation. His health practitioners were all on board to help him. Then, there was me, making every anti-cancer recipe on the planet. One family member jokingly called me, "The Soup Lady".

Richard often told us, "No matter the outcome, it's a win/win for me. If I live, that's great. If I don't, my kids will be waiting for me in heaven."

On Thanksgiving Day, November 27, 2014, at 11:11 p.m., he entered heaven, rejoicing into the arms of Jesus and, I'm certain, our children were waiting, with arms wide open.

There was a day when people called us Ken and Barbie. Apparently, most thought we were a couple who had it all together. But, I can't lie to you. We had our share of challenges in our marriage, especially during the last three years, before his death. We had a lot of fighting and confusion, as to why our life turned out the way it did. I wouldn't change a thing about any of it, because we loved each other, deeply, for 33 years. He was, and will always be, my soulmate and the father to our children. Sometimes, love can get ugly, but we never stopped honoring our time together. The next phase of my life will have to be another book,

Now, I'm a Widow ... Lord, Are You Kidding Me!

It's difficult to wake up from a nightmare, If you're not even asleep

Chapter 8

BEYOND THE NIGHTMARES

"But those who hope in the Lord will renew their strength. They will soar on wings like eagles; they will run and not grow weary, they will walk and not be faint." Isaiah 40:31

In early December, just two weeks after Richard passed, his cell phone rang. It was the District Attorney's office, wanting to discuss Mikey's murder case.

"Hello, is this Mrs. Portaro? My name is Robert Daskas, from the DA's office. I am handling your son's murder trial."

"Yes, I have heard your name from Richard. What can I do for you?"

"Is Richard available to talk?"

"I am sure you haven't heard, but Richard passed away two weeks ago, Robert."

"I am so sorry. I did not know. Should I call another family member? I was wondering who will be representing your family at the trial. It begins on February 12, 2015."

Richard had always attended these hearings to protect me. He knew I didn't want to hear the details. I only wanted Mikey to receive justice. Now, Richard was gone. *What in the heck do you want from me now, God? This is unbelievable, now this!*

"Hello, Mrs. Portaro, are you still there?"

"Yes, I'm sorry, this just hit me hard and my mind drifted elsewhere. I will represent Mikey on behalf of my family, Robert. Please send me any details I will need to be present."

"Again, Mrs. Portaro, I am truly very sorry for all that you have been through. I admire your courage."

"It's not so much courage, Robert, it's Faith."

And faith it took! Shortly after the call from Robert, a young lady phoned me. "Hi Momma P, this is Chelsea Garvin."

Chelsea graduated high school with Mikey and they were friends all throughout their school years. I remember thinking, how sweet of her to check up on me. "Hi honey, how are you?"

"I am calling you regarding Mikey's trial."

"What, why?"

"I work for the courthouse, and they selected me to be your trial advocate. I am appointed to make sure you don't see or hear anything that would be too difficult for you to handle. Kind of like Poppa P did."

See or hear anything too difficult? What did they expect this poor girl to do, blindfold me and apply earmuffs? I laughed inside knowing God was showing his presence, yet again. "Honey, you may think the courthouse appointed you, but I know, our higher court appointed you."

When God walks us through something in life, I believe, He'll show His presence, reminding us we can do all things through Him who strengthens us. I hung up the phone, thanking God for Chelsea, as I knew right there, He would be working on our behalf. She was definitely my guardian angel throughout the trial. At times, I could feel her holding my hand even when she wasn't.

Shortly before the trial began; I received a call from Frank Coumou, Chief Deputy District Attorney. I had known Frank, and his ex-wife, Susan, one of my dearest friends, for more than 25 years. My son, Joey, grew up with their son, Johan, and they were as close as blood brothers, and Johan called me, "Aunt Cynthia". When Johan lost his battle to cancer and entered Heaven in January 2018, many friends who knew the kids personalities would say, "Oh boy, there's a lot of fun and laughter going on in Heaven right now." And, I'm sure God did have his hands full with Mikey, Chrissy, and Johan – they were some fun crazy kids.

Frank Coumou said, "Hi, Cynthia. How are you doing? I'm so sorry about your loss of Richard."

I said, "Thank you, Frank. I appreciate your thoughtfulness. Is this about the trial?"

"Yes, I decided to handle the case for you, since I have such a personal interest. I want to fight for your family and find this kid guilty. We have enough evidence to seek the death penalty."

I am not sure what went through my mind, but I remember feeling sad. Death had become such a real and traumatic thing to me and my family over the past few years, it felt odd for someone to be seeking it. I thanked him and said, "I guess I'll see you on the 12th."

As I hung up the phone, I began to think about how God was covering and protecting my family throughout all the events we'd encountered over the past few years. First, there were the lead homicide detectives, Dean Raetz and Dean Kelly. We met them a few times during the hunt for Mikey's killer. The first, I recall, was in our family room. They assured us they were on Mikey's case, having a personal interest, because of church affiliation and knowing the killer's reputation. There's no way to describe how, during this entire ordeal, I felt confident they would, in fact, find this ungodly monster of a man guilty.

Then, there was Chelsea, appointed by the court to ensure I didn't see or hear anything too difficult. And now, Frank, our family friend, was ready to legally represent us in court.

TRIAL DAY 1

February 12, 2015, 10:00 a.m. began day one of the trial. My body, shaking like an earthquake, hitting record scales. I knew I was sitting in this chair, but my spirit was wandering elsewhere. All four attorneys from the defense and prosecutors gave their personal condolences to me, my family and friends, along with whoever else was present. I remember, of course, my Mom with me every moment, along with my friends, Robyn and Doris. Two of Mikey's best friends came several days to support us, James and Scott. They made it a point to bring me a little laughter, with some of their Mikey P stories. And, then there was my dear friend, Vicky, who was there every single day of the trial. I thank God for constantly surrounding me, both spiritually and physically, through the course of the trial.

The defense attorney, Joseph Abood, said such kind things to me before the trial began. I will never forget how his words of human kindness made me feel very comforted, well, as comforted as a Mother could, having faced such a tremendous, unexpected loss.

Then, all at once, I felt slapped in the face with the reality of Mikey's brutal murderer, as *he* entered the room. Dressed in a suit, prison guard alongside him, Brandon Jovan Hill walked into the courtroom. The young, black man, who murdered my son. He looked directly into my eyes, that penetrated my soul, with the feelings of anger arising.

"How can you look at me with that gaze, like you're some innocent boy?" I thought.

The judge told him what charges were brought against him and asked him how he pleaded. The two words that left his mouth shot through me like poisonous darts, "Not Guilty."

I ran out of the courtroom, with tears streaming down my face, sick to my stomach and my body filled with fear. *Can he even do that? What if they found him not guilty? Lord, how can I do this or expect my frail Mother to endure this with me?* Jurors were standing in the hallway, witnessing my display of sobs, after hearing this young man plead not guilty. I looked directly at them, took a few long deep breaths and spoke out loud, "Lord, please help me!"

The jury entered the room through a back door, and it seemed like forever for them to take their seats. When they settled, the judge started with her instructions to them.

"Just keep breathing," I thought, as I sat silently, breathing in and out, my eyes fixed on the back of my son's killer's head. *"Just keep breathing, Cynthia. Breathe in the breath of God, He is here with you ... I hope!"*

The assistant District Attorney, Richard Scow, started opening remarks. He affirmed, without a shadow of a doubt, Brandon J. Hill was guilty of Mikey's murder. He explained how Mikey was out selling tickets for his concert the evening of March 30th. Mikey and his partner, Jeff, had formed a music group together, called Ekoh. They wrote their own music, did hip hop dance, rapped and sang, to a crowd of thousands. During the course of being out selling tickets to the event, Mikey received a call from a friend, Ashley Lare. Together, they made a to meet in between their locations, so she could purchase some tickets. They decided upon Tenaya Creek at 11:00 p.m.

"There were a lot of details spoken as to where Michael parked his car, how he stepped out to talk with Ashley and exchange tickets for money." Scow said, as he turned back to the video surveillance from the scene, "Michael walks back to his car, gets into the car, but doesn't close his door immediately."

Scow then described how you see the hooded figure, smoking a cigarette, walking toward the car at 11:14 p.m. "Hill was walking toward the back of Michael's car, and within eight seconds, you can see him throw down the cigarette, start shooting, then something falls to the ground, it's kind of big, and it stays there." He circled Mikey's body on the video surveillance, "Showing the large dark object, not moving, while his car pulled away about 30 seconds later."

I remember, he said, from video surveillance, Mikey was shot precisely at 11:16 p.m., on March 30, 2011.

He then showed an enlarged photograph of the parking lot. "What you see on the ground," Scow continued, "within those eight seconds, is Michael Portaro, and he does not move. The autopsy, performed the next day, showed he was shot, at an extremely close range, from his back, four times. One in

68

the left neck, one in the back of the head on his right side and two in the back that had exit wounds."

"Shot four times, and this is how he's left and found already dead in the parking lot, while the suspect drives away with Mikey's car." I took another breath in and out. *"And he pleaded not guilty?"*

Richard Scow continues, "As the crime scene analysts are going through the scene, they document everything. They collect what may, even what may not, have been relevant, just what may help further their investigation about who did this assassination, execution style."

"Execution style! Don't forget that, Mr. I'm Not Guilty." I thought, as Scow continued his case.

One of the items collected was a cigarette butt, that was under Mikey's leg in the middle of the parking lot, left undisturbed. It had burned down to the filter, leaving a burned hole in Mikey's light black jeans.

As Scow covers every single detail I thought, *"God, I know you are here with us...I hope."*

Some of the details were somewhat confusing to me. If Mikey was shot on March 30, why was his death certificate dated March 31, with no time on it? I was later informed, it was when the coroner officially declared him dead. Too many thoughts were racing through my mind, battling to be present during the course of the trial. At some points, all I wanted was to run away from my life and find a quiet place to hibernate.

I know my spirit was somewhere else during the trial, because, although I was journaling everything that has been written thus far, I do not remember even having my journal with me through the trial. I didn't realize I had been writing, until I started reading through my journals these past nine years of writing.

On the second day of the trial I wrote: God's got this!

Mikey always said that to me, "Mom ... I got this!"

After Scow's opening statements, the Assistant Defense Attorney, Christy Craig, didn't have much to defend. In her opening statement; she was totally trying to confuse the jury. She said, "Now, what concerns me is, we're talking about the death of a young man and it's a tragic thing. It's natural, it's human, and you wouldn't be a normal person, if you didn't feel compassion and sympathy for what happened to him, for his family or for the people who loved him. But, the Judge has made it clear, and we're asking you to set the compassion and sympathy aside, as you listen to the evidence that's presented to you."

"Set compassion and sympathy aside?" I thought, *"They already saw the evidence. What more is there to see? I don't like her at all, at all! Can I escape now?"*

Frank Coumou began reading from the detective's investigation notes, "On March 24, he wrote to some female in his Facebook messenger, *Ain't shit wrong that .357 can't handle. Feel me.* On March 31, at 11:47 a.m., Hill writes, *Bros, you already know I'm a FUX with you. I just ain't mobile.* That's on the morning of Mikey's death. He's carrying a .357 and he doesn't have a car anymore. On April 1, at 7:24 he posts, *I'm smoking two best friends, LOL. I'm back on deck with the bomb best friend."*

70

This kid is really screwed up. I wrote in my journal, **How is anyone, raised to be such a monster? No remorse of just killing a beautiful soul ... just wants to keep himself high. Who was he looking to kill next?**

There were more posts from Hill, the DA went through. The real joy was listening to Frank saying, "On May 12, his sister says: *I just seen you on the news, WTF. I didn't know they released the video.* Hill says, *Whoo-hoo. The homey makes the news. Type of big shit SMH,* (shaking my head) *that's hella deep. LOL Ha, Ha, Ha, Ha, I'm famous, bitches. LOL.*"

The first witness called to the stand was Elvis Canamero. Elvis was robbed by Hill, just two weeks prior to Mikey's murder. The Defense Attorney fearlessly worked, trying to get him to say, maybe he forgot. He was working it, trying to discredit him as a witness. All this, even though Elvis had identified Hill from a line-up of six men, all looking similar to Hill.

It was horrible to listen and watch. *"OMG ... this man's head was held at gunpoint by Hill ... Elvis somehow managed to flee the car and run for his life ... I doubt he would forget what he looked like, especially now staring at Hill in the face, inside the courtroom."*

I do remember thinking they said Elvis's car was recovered at Alexander Garden Apartments, about a mile away from Tenaya Creek around 12:00 pm, March 30, 2011. Mikey, Elvis, they weren't the only people Brandon Jovan Hill had assaulted. They were only a few of the many prior convictions on Hill's record, of hurting people and robbing them. Since 2008, he had been in and out of jail, on multiple charges. And, the DA's office was sure to bring that to light.

My spirit left the courtroom again ... as I silently sat numb, still staring at the back of Hill's head. *Why won't he stop turning around and looking at me with his cold dark eyes?*

A new witness took the stand. Steve Grady found Mikey's car in a dump, the next day, where he worked at North 3rd Street and Mayflower. Hill had burned the interior of the car, so Mr. Grady phoned the North Las Vegas Fire Department. The Fire Department had taken pictures at the scene, which were used in the courtroom.

His license plate, **MIKEY P**, was pictured on a very large screen. My eyes swelled up and tears rolled down my cheeks. They were those uncontrollable tears, forming in the back of my throat, that became uncontainable. I keep his duplicate license plate in my garden of memories, along with the front grill of his Altima. Then, one of the photos showed several items burned on the seats.

Remember, in the first chapter, I wrote Mikey had written a song for me, he was planning to dedicate and sing it to me during his Thursday, March 31 performance? He had sung it to me previously over the phone, as I cried and felt my heart bursting with pride. He said, "Well ... you are my Shero Momma!" Now, knowing Hill burned Mikey's belongings, left in the car, I became even angrier with the kid. *I'll never ever have those lyrics to be sung to me. Never have them to treasure. They're nothing but ashes ... like his body is to me today.* My heart ached. *He dumped his car like he dumped my son's body.*

I ran out of the courtroom, before I broke down or fainted. The Judge ordered a 10-minute recess for Mrs. Portaro to regain herself.

10 minutes? How about 10 years to regain myself.

We re-entered the courtroom, and several minutes later, a new witness was called to the stand. Todd, a patrol officer. He described how Mr. Hill was discovered on April 10, 2011 at 12:18 a.m, by his team of dogs. When they sniffed Mr. Hill out of the bushes, Hill identified himself. He was read his rights and then, due to the many prior warrants, was arrested. Officer Daniel, from Las Vegas Metropolitan Police, Canine Unit, concurred with those events. A few days after his arrest, someone posted bail for Hill.

Then there was Chelsea, a CSI Agent. She took the stand and informed us Hill's DNA was found on March 04, 2011, during a robbery investigation. Hill was arrested and, again, let out on bail.

Why can't we keep criminals in jail? I felt annoyed and saddened, all at the same time, *Mikey, and so many others, would be alive today.*

She continued, proving the DNA was a match to the DNA found on a cigarette butt under Mikey's leg discovered at the scene of the murder. Apparently, Hill threw it down before he shot Mikey to his death. Hill sat through these accusations, with a cold look in his eyes, still not showing any sign of remorse.

Randall, Las Vegas Metropolitan Police, CSI Agent, Firearms Unit, was next to take the stand.

I took some stress relief oil out of my purse, *Essential Oil Time, breathing in the breath of God.*

Randall spoke with such control and strength, "The firearm, 357 Magnum, found where Hill was arrested on May 19, 2011, is a definite match to the bullets recovered from Mr. Portaro's body. The match result is found to be 600 times accurate to the gun and the bullets.

At some point during his delivery, I remember thinking, *I wish it were me instead. Why, my son? Mikey would have given him the car, that's who he was.*

The jurors, after hearing witnesses speak on the stand, were given the opportunity to ask questions. One of the questions they asked Randall left me completely dumbfounded, "Are you sure the bullets match the gun?"

Randall surprisingly looked at the Jury and said, and again, an extremely strong response, "Did you not hear what I said? 600 times, an accurate match!"

Our two God-sent Lead Homicide Detectives, Dean Raetz and Dean Kelly, sat next to me. I remember having a feeling of comfort and safety from their presence next to me in the courtroom. They both had worked this case diligently, while paying special attention to all the details.

One of them was called to the witness stand. Dean Raetz spoke of the blood found on Hill's white sneakers, while searching his apartment. The blood from his shoes was 1/650-billion match, to Mikey's.

I seriously can't believe I have the strength to write and live through this nightmare. I have to take a break and go cry again. I wrote in my journal.

We all pretty much had a lot of tears welling up and trying to hold them back ... was impossible!

Two weeks of enduring this trauma to the soul, I think it became too much for me emotionally, writing any more details, as my journal notes began trailing off. Now, the jury was to leave and return with their verdict. The Nevada State District Attorney's office was seeking the death penalty. This became the most real of anything our family had ever witnessed. I was approached by the State, Frank and Richard, and asked if I would speak to the court. "The jury needs to hear what effect this tragedy has had on you and your family."

The strength it took to speak at my kid's memorials was one thing. I was in shock back then ... how was I supposed to muster up the strength to do this?

Chapter 9

THE VERDICT

"Rejoice, you nations, with his people, for he will avenge the blood of his servants; he will take vengeance on his enemies and make atonement for his land and people." Deuteronomy 32:43

Jury Trial - Day 8
Friday, February 20, 2015.

The Judge requested Hill and his counsel, "Please stand. The clerk will now read the verdict out loud."

This was the moment we had been waiting for, almost four years.

"We, the jury in the above titled case, find the defendant, Brandon Jovan Hill, as follows:

Count 1, Robbery with Use of a Deadly Weapon: Not guilty

Count 2, Grand Larceny, Auto: Not guilty

County 3, Robbery with Use of a Deadly Weapon: GUILTY of Robbery with Use of a Deadly Weapon.

Count 4, Grand Larceny, Auto: GUILTY of Grand Larceny Auto

Count 5, Murder with Use of a Deadly Weapon: GUILTY of First-Degree Murder with Use of a deadly weapon, answering the following: 12, number of jurors who find the murder was willful, deliberate, and premeditated. 12, number of jurors who find the murder was committed during the perpetration or attempt at perpetration of robbery.

Count 6, Carrying Concealed Fireman: Guilty of Carrying Concealed Firearm."

"Okay folks," the Judge addressed the jury, "thank you very much for your time and attention, so far. Now, as mentioned during jury selection, there will be a penalty phase, because we have had a conviction of first-degree murder."

The Judge addressed the entire courtroom. "We will pick up with that part on Monday at 1:00 p.m. Enjoy your weekend, and we'll see you then."

"Enjoy your weekend," I thought, "Yeah right! We still had an entire weekend before we'd find out whether or not he'd receive the death penalty."

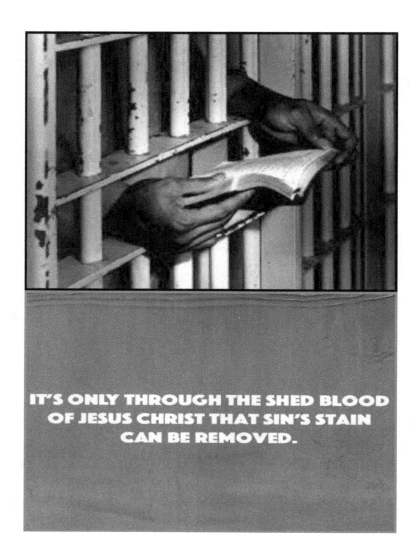

IT'S ONLY THROUGH THE SHED BLOOD
OF JESUS CHRIST THAT SIN'S STAIN
CAN BE REMOVED.

Chapter 10

WHEN GOD SPEAKS

To open their eyes and turn them from darkness to light, from the power of Satan to God, so that they may receive forgiveness of sins and a place among those who are sanctified by faith in me. Acts 26:18 (NIV)

Jury Trial - Day 9
Monday, February 23, 2015.

The act of forgiveness is spoken frequently in the Bible. The word "forgive" appears 42 times in the Old Testament and 33 times in the New Testament. The word "forgiven" appears 17 times in the Old Testament and 28 times in the New Testament. And the word "Forgiving" appears six times in the Old Testament and one time in the New. Those numbers can vary from different translations of the Bible.

Forgiving is deemed to set the captive free. During the course of the trial, the captive was me. Many thoughts surrounding forgiveness bounced through my head:

Forgive that you may be forgiven, healed, and restored.

Forgiveness is more for us, than for those we are asked to forgive.

So, if I profess to be a Christian, who loves God with all my mind, heart, soul and spirit, then should I not forgive even my son's killer?

Just thinking about this again, five years after the trial, makes me tremble, and my heart well with tears.

On the day the jury was to deliver the sentence, I was getting dressed, after spending a very long time in prayer, crying out to God. I wanted justice but had this burden of all the lessons I'd ever read or heard about forgiveness, weighing in my soul. The thoughts racing through my mind were uncontrollably difficult and being torn in way too many directions. How could I forgive the unbearable?

I thought about Jesus on the Cross, when Jesus prayed, *"Father, forgive them; they don't know what they're doing." Luke 23:34 (MSG)*

Here was my leader, forgiving the unforgivable, how can I consider myself His, if I choose not to forgive this killer. "God help me ... what do I do?"

I was sitting at my make-up mirror, applying makeup, (why bother ... right?) and I audibly heard God speak to me. This was the second time I audibly heard God speak to me. The first was about a school my son was to attend entering seventh grade and it worked out for the good of our entire family. But, on this day, He spoke these words that were much harder to hear, "Daughter, I am with you, here and always. Forgive him. Do not worry, worry is for Me. I am asking you to speak and **loudly**, in that courtroom. Remove the death penalty."

Sitting there frozen, I fell to the floor, my face buried in the bathroom floor rug, sobbing uncontrollably. "How ...

How... How can You expect me to do this? Lord, haven't I given enough, been through enough torture, haven't I been willing to endure this in your name?"

Again, my thoughts began to think of what Jesus did on the Cross for all of us. He was brutally broken, stabbed, mocked, whipped and hung to die, all while His mother watched her son being left to bleed to death. Why should our endurance as Christians, who claim to love Him so much, be any different? At that point, I called my sons – Rico and Joey – and asked them what they thought, after explaining what happened. They both agreed, we should remove the death penalty. Their agreement, in itself, was a confirmation of what needed to be done.

I arrived at the courthouse about 30 minutes before the sentencing was to begin. I recall taking a lot of very long, deep breaths during this entire process of the trial. I went up to Frank Coumou and asked if we could talk. Apparently, it is not allowed, unless the defense side is present as well. I told him that was fine. He walked up to the judge, with the defense attorney, Mr. Abood, and asked her if they could have 10 minutes to speak with me. They then took me into a small room, right outside the courtroom, with all four attorneys and a security guard. This did not go over so well with Mr. Coumou ....

"I want you to remove the death penalty!" I told Frank in a casual tone I'd deliver any other kind of news to him.

Frank shook his head in disbelief and shock. "You can't do that!"

"Yes, I can, and Yes, you will!"

"Why," Frank demanded, "Why, would you even think about doing that?"

"Well, Frank, you have known me for a very long time and you also know I am a woman of Faith and Justice. My family doesn't want another death on our hands. And ... God asked me to not only forgive him, but to remove the death penalty! Do you understand how difficult this has been for us?"

The three other attorneys looked at me in amazement, as Frank and I continued arguing a while longer.

"What! That is the most ridiculous request I have ever heard. I won't allow it; this is my case and my decision."

I knew what God had spoken to me and I refused to back down. "My son, my choice, and my flipping decision!" I stared Frank in the eyes, "Now, I want it off or I will go into that courtroom with every news station present and ask the judge to dismiss everything. This has been torture for my family and we want this over, for good!"

"Okay," Frank sighed in defeat, "you win."

"You mean, God won."

As we re-entered the courtroom, the attorneys approached the bench. I was later told Frank informed the Judge of our wishes for the defendant and my request for an opportunity to address the court.

The Judge said, "Of course. However, Mr. Hill will need to sign documents accepting the jury being let go and allow sentencing by the court."

There was a very long pause in the proceeding, before the Judge addressed everyone in the courtroom. "Folks, we've been discussing some procedural matters up on the bench. Go ahead, Mr. Coumou, how do you intend to proceed."

Frank Coumou stood to address the courtroom. "Yes, Your Honor. This morning, we were approached by the victim's family members, and they've made a request to have the Court do the sentencing. That would require the State to withdraw the notice to seek the death penalty, which is what the State was prepared to do, understanding we lost our first aggravator, we filed the notice on, and --- it remains two aggravators for us to proceed. Mrs. Portaro would now like to address the court."

"Can you state and spell your name for the record, Ma'am?"

"Cynthia Portaro." I stated and proceeded with the spelling. They thanked me and said go ahead. There was total silence in the room; you could hear a pin drop, as they say.

"It's been a grueling four years for our entire Portaro family, my surviving children, and our extended family. It is the desire of this family, being Christian-based believers; we would like to ask the Court not to pursue the death penalty. I'd like to leave it up to you and God to move forward on this. We just don't want another life taken. As my son Rico said, "We do not want to live the rest of our lives with this burden on us, too. On our behalf, we would like this removed."

As I spoke these words, Hill's family was weeping loudly. And, to my utter surprise; Hill stood up, looked directly at me, and said, "I want to say thank you for forgiving me. I'm sorry for everything that you've been through. If I could take it back, I would."

I responded, "I hope you find peace where you're going. You still have your life and a destiny to live."

All parties agreed to my request. Hill's attorney, Mr. Abood, looked at me and said, "We thank the Portaro family very much, and we will most certainly be signing stipulations and proceeding in this manner. Thank you."

After more conversations regarding this decision, the clerk addressed the courtroom. "Sentencing is April 16, 8:30 a.m."

Then the Jury was thanked and dismissed.

When we walked out of the courtroom, I was approached by Hill's family. News cameras everywhere, bombarding me, wanting an interview. I remember hugging his mother and grandmother, while still weeping, but more uncontrollably. I don't remember who said this to me, but she said, "We get to go visit Brandon, while your children are gone."

My friend, Vicky Quinn, recently told me I stopped everyone from talking, and said, "Let's just pray."

Through much of the trial, I felt like I was wandering in the desert with Moses, only frozen.

I believe, with all my heart and soul, this is exactly WWJD – What Would Jesus Do! When you are called to do the "Unthinkable" ...

What Would You Do?

Posted March 1, 2015 - 12:01 a.m.
EDITORIAL: The Power of Forgiveness
LAS VEGAS REVIEW-JOURNAL

Sometimes, a person does something so magnanimous and so unexpected that it can make even the most hardened soul have renewed faith in humanity. Cynthia Portaro delivered such a moment last week at the Regional Justice Center. Her actions were so moving that veteran public defender Joseph Abood said he'd, "Never seen anything like it."

On the night of March 30, 2011, Mrs. Portaro lost her 22-year-old son, Mike. He was in the parking lot of the Tenaya Creek Brewery, selling tickets to his hip-hop group's show, when he was shot to death.

Brandon Hill was convicted of the murder, as well as robbery with use of a deadly weapon and grand larceny auto. After initially denying all involvement in the crime, Hill, before the court, apologized to Mike Portaro's family.

Mrs. Portaro could have ignored him. She could have told him to burn in hell. Instead, she forgave him.

On Monday, Cynthia Portaro approached prosecutors, who were seeking the death penalty, and told them she did not want to see Hill executed. The district attorney's office honored her wishes, withdrew the death penalty and now plan to seek a sentence of life in prison without the possibility of parole.

"I got what I wanted — an apology from Brandon," Mrs. Portaro told the Review-Journal's David Ferrara. "I felt a sense of relief that there is no hatred, animosity, anger.

85

Because, if you live in Christ, you cannot live with those things."

But Mrs. Portaro's compassion is more remarkable than it appears. She lost another child, her daughter Christina, in an ATV crash the same year Mike was killed. Her husband, Richard, died on Thanksgiving last year. Despite this loss, she found it in her heart to accept an apology from the man who murdered her son — and spare his life.

"I personally didn't want to see another person die," Portaro said, before hugging members of Hill's family.

Those who support capital punishment, and those who have supported the executions of the killers of their loved ones, are not in the wrong. Capital punishment is not about revenge, and it certainly isn't a deterrent to murder. It's the ultimate public safety measure — it's about making absolutely certain a convicted killer can never harm anyone again.

That said, the public would also be a lot safer if everyone had the grace and gravitas of Cynthia Portaro.

They said...
"Write the longest sentence you know."
I wrote:
"A life without You."
Cameron Lincoln

Chapter 11

THE LIFE SENTENCE

"Blessed is the one who perseveres under trial, because having stood the test, that person will receive the crown of life that the Lord has promised to those who love Him." James 1:12

We returned to the courtroom for one final time, on Thursday, April 16, 2015, for sentencing. Because the death sentence was no longer an option, Frank Coumou began by requesting the court to impose life without the possibility of parole. "Mr. Hill had every opportunity on March 30 to make the right decision and let Michael go. Just let him enjoy the liberty that every law-abiding citizen of this country has. The opportunity to get back in his car, leave, and go home to his family. But, instead, Mr. Hill chose on the moment, which he had plenty of time to think about, while smoking his cigarette, to sneak up with a loaded revolver and take the life of Michael Portaro. It's so unfortunate, because Michael was a very productive member of society. He came from a good family. They taught him the right ways to live and abide by the law. I can tell you from my own personal contact through somebody close to me, he even told me that Michael was the type of person that would counsel other younger kids about drugs and staying away from alcohol, because that was important to him. Michael graduated from high school. He was a star football player. He was also on the basketball team. He went to college, where he received a scholarship to play football. And, as you know, he was trying to promote and get into the music industry. He was doing everything right, everything that you as a parent would want to see your child do, and on this particular night, somebody decided that he was not worthy of living. They robbed him of his hopes, and dreams, along with his future away from him and his family."

Mr. Coumou proceeded with Hill's criminal background and pretty much covered all that had been discovered during the trial. He addressed the fact that Mr. Hill was a known member of The Gerson Park Kingmen Gang. Always packing his gun during every arrest, fully loaded mind you. He continued on to explain how Mr. Hill was always packing a fully loaded gun, even during his arrest. Then, Mr. Coumou went on to review how Hill's crimes of late had escalated into, now, more serious and violent ones ... as in the death of Michael Portaro.

Ultimately, Mr. Coumou was pursuing a life in prison for Mr. Hill. Our family will always be grateful how he and Richard Scow defended Mikey with the honor, dignity and truth he deserved. This prosecution obviously did not take place overnight. They all cared enough about my family to prepare every detail of this case for years to prove without a doubt, Branden Jovan Hill, was guilty and is off the streets.

The defense attorney, Mr. Abood, stood up after Frank finished, "Mr. Hill would like to have the opportunity to speak on his behalf."

Hill proceeded with these words. "I am not going to make excuses for what I did. You know, I really am sorry to the family. If I could take it back, it wouldn't have ever happened. To my family, to drag them through this, you know, like the DA just said, my whole life I've been making bad choices. Unfortunately, it led to this. That's not who I am. I'm not a monster, you know. I'm really sorry for what happened. I mean, my words can't get him back, but if it was possible, I'd give my own life. I got a son, you know. I don't know how I would feel if somebody did that to him. The time I've been here, I've thought about it every day. I'm not who the DA said I am. I mean, the way I grew up is. I am not going to make excuses, but I am not that same person any more. I'm just asking, I know I am going to prison, but I'm just asking you don't send me away forever. Gimme some chance to get my life back. somewhere down the road. That's it."

"WOW ... how does a mother of a murdered son feel about his request? Why shouldn't he go away for life? Mikey doesn't have that opportunity. His family doesn't have that opportunity. Why him? I know God told me to forgive him and I did. However, forgiveness doesn't magically take away all the very real human emotions one experiences during this kind of tribulation."

Ms. Craig, Hill's other attorney, stood to address the court once Hill sat down. "Mr. Hill shouldn't serve life without parole." She went on to tell how he's going to spend decades of his life in jail, no matter what the decision is, life with the possibility or life without the possibility. Frankly, it's appropriate, given the loss of Michael Portaro's life, that Mr. Hill spends time in prison. It's the punishment that comes with his decision to rob and kill, it's what he deserves. It's what he accepts, and he does think about it every day.

So, again, they continued to defend why Hill should have the ability to have parole.

"OMG..." I thought, *"give it a rest already."*

She asked the court to consider the idea mercy plays a role. Hill should have the idea there's hope. He can go to school in prison, he can work in prison, and he can become a role model to others. Let him have his possibility of redemption.

Redemption .... Sure, when my family receives it.

Then it was my turn to address the court once more. I was asked to raise my right hand and say my name, again, for the court.

"Cynthia Portaro."

"You may proceed."

"Before I go through the..." Choking tears through the words I spoke, "I'm sorry this is going to be difficult. I will get through this, because I've walked the journey of great loss over the last four years. I have been waiting for this day and this moment in time, that Mikey's life would be honored, for whom he was, and not for how his life was taken. While Mr. Hill was in jail these past four years, pondering what he had done, I don't think anybody really understands the devastation happening in a family, when a life is taken away, senselessly and brutally. I don't know what he was thinking. I don't know if he was on drugs. I don't know if his heart is numb. I don't know anything other than what my family has endured, for four years of hopelessness on a daily basis. Mikey was more than just a 23-year-old ... well he wasn't even 23 yet. He would have been 23 on May 25, 2011. Mr. Hill turned 23 on June 18' but not Mikey. If I look at the lives of my son and Brandon, they're obviously the exact same age, exactly one month apart. I think my husband, and I, were able to raise a son of compassion for others. I say that, because later on I will share pictures, to show the court, to give you all a little piece of the life Mikey lived. He was the kid at school who stuck up for the bullied. He wouldn't ever mind, if he were the one who got into trouble, protecting the kids who were bullied. That was his personality, that's who Mikey was. He was a positive, motivating kid. He motivated the football team. He walked around with positive motivational quotes in his pocket. He would read to keep him going in a very tuff society. There was a time in his high school football career, he didn't think he was going to make the level he wanted. We were always a family of, you could do it; you can be who God intended you to be. You can be whoever you choose to be, but you've got to make the effort. You've got to put in the work; you've got to get the grades.

And, to be honest with you, Mike, had a little bit of a fork in the road, when he was 16-years-old. He didn't get into big trouble, but he was at a party and the party got busted. It was the fork in the road, where we told Mike, it's always going to be about the choices you make. One of the things that I always told our children – and we raised five – when they left the house, I would make them repeat back to me, "I will make good choices, wear my seatbelt and watch out for assholes." Apparently, I didn't get to say that to Mikey that dark night, (looking at Hill now), "You being the asshole. I'm sorry, but that's the choice this man made."

I showed some family photos and explained what each one meant to our family. To give a little background, I began to explain this ... "Mikey was my ninth pregnancy. It took a lot of endurance to give birth to him, with all the complications I had carrying him. When Mikey was seven weeks old, he was diagnosed with a heart defect. He had two open heart surgeries at UCLA Medical Center. There were two babies, with the exact same surgeries, at the same time. The others died, same defect, same age. I told God that day, if he let Mikey live, *'we would raise him up in the way he should go, so when he became old, he would not depart from his belief.'*[2] I am quoting from the book of Proverbs. Mikey's whole thing was ... he would say ... 'Mom, I think I have such a purpose, with such a tender heart for people, because of what I went through. Because of what our family went through to have me. I appreciate how you taught me to fight for what my destiny is.' Mikey was so proud of the scars on his chest from his surgery."

I shared about his best friend, Andy, and how my friend, Vicky, sitting in the courtroom, had a son with the same disability. I also shared the letter from Andy's parents about what Mikey meant to them. These letters really described who my son was to many people ... not just our family. I showed a picture of his memorial balloon release, where 1,100 hundred people showed up. I explained how I found a probationary employee report from his employer. His words about Mikey were this: knowledgeable, outstanding quantity of work, cooperation, conduct, interpersonal skills, and attitude toward job, punctuality and great work. He signed it exceptional; you'll be getting a raise. I went on about his relationship with his siblings, especially Chrissy.

At one point, I turned to Hill and said, "If you knew Mike, as the friend he was to many, you would not have ever done this to him or our family. He would have given you his car, his money, the shirt off his back and brought you home to

---

[2] **Proverbs 22:6**

his family to be cared for, just as he always had done so many times in his life."

I closed with this, "People lose children every day. None are immune to such devastation. When you talk about a life sentence, we have that sentence. We are sentenced, for life, without our key family members. I didn't make a bad choice, I didn't cause any of this to happen, but I'm sentenced to a life of grief ... and *without* the chance of parole ... by the way!"

I addressed the Judge, "Your Honor, thank you for giving me the time that you have. I am in agreement with whatever you come up with for sentencing."

I returned to my seat. The intensity in the courtroom became so real. We could finally close this door and move on with our lives. All we needed was the Judge's verdict. There was a very long pause in proceeding, then Judge Caddish began speaking.

"All right ... To call this situation a tragedy, really doesn't seem to capture what happened here for so many people, unfortunately. For Mr. Portaro to have lost his life senselessly, and the circumstance, when he did nothing wrong, certainly to deserve that or his family, certainly, and friends and those whose lives he touched, certainly didn't deserve what happened that day. And, similarly, your family members and supporters who are here in large numbers to support you, didn't deserve to be in this situation and to watch what's going on here today, Mr. Hill, and those are a result of choices you made. No one else in the courtroom got to make the choice that day, only you did."

"After multiple arrests, with weapons involved, to still have escalated and violently taken the life of this young person, who was the same age as you, is, you know, it's an awful situation that is obvious and, again, it just doesn't seem to adequately describe what happened here. And, for the two of you to be the same age and have your lives intersect that day and for Mr. Portaro to have lost his life and, obviously, your life is never going to be the same again either, nor will your family and friends and those who support you."

"I recognize, certainly, your life growing up is different from the life Mr. Portaro had growing up. It's certainly not an excuse for what happened here, but I do recognize the different background and circumstances that you faced. But, ultimately, it's the choices you made as an adult that brought us here today."

"I appreciate the reasons for the State seeking life without possibility of parole in the circumstance, the multiple arrests, convictions; and time served for weapons-related offenses that preceded this offense. I also see that Mr. Hill was a young man, still is a young man, and at the time of this offense, had no prior felonies, no prior crimes of violence. He had weapons, certainly, but as far as I'm aware, this is the first time when one was used, based on what's before me."

"Obviously I sure hope it's the last. And, it is concerning that, after this offense, the comments you were making in communications you were having, still don't seem remorseful for what occurred. And, if there was an incident in the jail after that, a violent incident, this is not a good sign. However, when I look at you as a young man having done this at age 22, now 26, and looking at, you know, these choices that were made from 18 to 22 years old, I would hope at least by the time you're in your 50s or 60s, something might have changed, so you might not be a danger in the community, as you were during the period of time shown on the chart, submitted by the State. I don't feel, today, I can say there will never be a day that you would be safe to be in the community."

"And, so, recognizing the seriousness and impact of this crime and you being the one who made the choices that day, I still believe a possibility of parole is appropriate; at some point, if you do the right things, if you're not getting in fights and getting in trouble in prison, you might someday, when you're much older than you are today, persuade a parole board that you would not be a danger to the community, if you were released on supervision on parole."

She then went onto a list of fees, charges, and time to be served. Among them, being the charges regarding Mikey's murder: "On Count 5, murder with use of a deadly weapon, sentencing you to life with the possibility of parole after 20 years; for the use of a deadly weapon in that offense, which obviously is what caused this tragic death to occur, a consecutive sentence of 240 months in Nevada Department of Corrections, minimum parole eligibility after 96 months, concurrent with Count 4."

The Judge ended the list with her final verdict, "I believe that given that they're running concurrent, and to announce the aggregate sentence, so it's life, plus 20 years, with minimum parole eligibility after 28 years, and 1,429 days credit, for time served."

"Mr. Hill, the rest will be up to you, on how you behave in prison. If you don't cooperate, you will spend the rest of your life in prison. Maybe someday, 25, 30 years down the road, if you prove yourself worthy, you could potentially be paroled. I hope that you will work to do good in prison, so you will earn that right, at some point, or that opportunity, at some point."

While Hill's family wept loudly in the courtroom, I was silently rejoicing. I felt a sense of peace and relief he was going away for a very long time, to hopefully someday be a compassionate member of society. I did not feel sorry for him, thinking of why he's imprisoned for a very long time. Life is about having Faith to Grow in Christ, and to Serve others while he's away. I have prayed God gets a hold of him, and his thoughts of what he did, for a very long time. God is always good to answer them, in His perfect timing.

Even though our family will never be the same, we still celebrate life's precious moments. Birthdays and holidays are felt with emptiness but, we are grateful to share family time. My son, Joey, recently was engaged to a beautiful young lady, Kellie, who we all love dearly. She has already become family to all of us. Yes, we think about our losses every single day. However, those losses do not define us; they bring us hope in Christ and eternity, knowing we will see them again.

Killer gets lighter sentence after appeal by victim's mother

By DAVID FERRARA

LAS VEGAS REVIEW-JOURNAL

A man who once faced the death penalty for fatally shooting 22-year-old Mike Portaro will get a chance at parole, a judge decided Thursday.

Brandon Hill was convicted earlier this year in the March 2011 slaying outside the Tenaya Creek Brewery at 3101 N. Tenaya Way. After the jury reached its decision, Portaro's mother, Cynthia Portaro, told prosecutors she did not want to see Hill put to death.

After a lengthy sentencing hearing Thursday, at which both Portaro and Hill spoke, District Judge Elissa Cadish ordered Hill to serve 28 years to life in prison.

Cynthia Portaro called the sentence "light," but said she was glad the criminal case against Hill was finished.

Hill apologized to Portaro after the jury verdict and at the sentencing.

"My words can't give them their loved one back," he said. "But if it was possible I'd give my own life."

Five months after Mike Portaro died, his sister Christina Portaro was killed in an ATV crash. Their father, Richard Portaro, Cynthia Portaro's husband, died on Thanksgiving last year.

At Hill's trial, prosecutors showed jurors surveillance video from the brew pub's parking lot that appeared to show a young man wearing a hooded sweatshirt and white shoes and smoking a cigarette. They also presented evidence that tied Hill to Mike Portaro's slaying; a cigarette found outside the bar that had Hill's DNA, Portaro's blood on Hill's shoes, the gun used in the slaying that was recovered near Hill during an April arrest and forensic evidence found in Portaro's car, which was stolen the night he was killed.

At the hearing Thursday, Cynthia Portaro spoke of the impact of first losing a son, then a daughter and her husband.

"I have that life sentence," she said. "I am sentenced to live without my family; I didn't cause any of this to happen, but I am sentenced to a life of grief."

After her son was slain, Cynthia Portaro started Mourning Hope of Las Vegas, a support group to help herself and others cope with the loss of loved ones. The faith-based group meets at the International Church of Las Vegas, 8100 Westcliff Drive.

Since speaking out against the death penalty after Hill's trial, Portaro has been invited to forums about capital punishment, including one at UNLV earlier this week. She plans to attend a Death Penalty Focus ceremony in Beverly Hills, Calif., next month.

Members of Hill's family said they wanted to reach out to Portaro after the trial and express their sympathy.

"There's nothing I could say to her to apologize," said Hill's sister, Talarisha, as she cried. "I get to go see him. She's got her baby in a grave."

Contact reporter David Ferrara at dferrara@reviewjournal.com or 702-380-1039. Find him on Twitter: @randompoker

Posted March 1, 2015 - 12:01am
EDITORIAL: The power of forgiveness
LAS VEGAS REVIEW-JOURNAL

Sometimes, a person does something so magnanimous and so unexpected that it can make even the most hardened soul have renewed faith in humanity. Cynthia Portaro delivered such a moment last week at the Regional Justice Center. Her actions were so moving that veteran public defender Joseph Abood said he'd "never seen anything like it."

On the night of March 30, 2011, Mrs. Portaro lost her 22-year-old son, Mike. He was in the parking lot of the Tenaya Creek Brewery, selling tickets to his hip-hop group's show, when he was shot to death.

Brandon Hill was convicted of the murder, as well as robbery with use of a deadly weapon and grand larceny auto. After initially denying all involvement in the crime, Hill, before the court, apologized to Mike Portaro's family.

Mrs. Portaro could have ignored him. She could have told him to burn in hell. Instead, she forgave him.

On Monday, Cynthia Portaro approached prosecutors, who were seeking the death penalty, and told them she did not want to see Hill executed. The district attorney's office honored her wishes, withdrew the death penalty and now plan to seek a sentence of life in prison without the possibility of parole.

"I got what I wanted — an apology from Brandon," Mrs. Portaro told the Review-Journal's David Ferrara. "I felt a sense of relief that there is no hatred, animosity, anger. Because if you live in Christ, you cannot live with those things."

But Mrs. Portaro's compassion is more remarkable than it appears. She lost another child, her daughter Christina, in an ATV crash the same year Mike was killed. Her husband, Richard, died on Thanksgiving last year. Despite this loss, she found it in her heart to accept an apology from the man who murdered her son — and spare his life.

"I personally didn't want to see another person die," Portaro said before hugging members of Hill's family.

Those who support capital punishment, and those who have supported the executions of the killers of their loved ones, are not in the wrong. Capital punishment is not about revenge, and it certainly isn't a deterrent to murder. It's the ultimate public safety measure — it's about making absolutely certain a convicted killer can never harm anyone again.

That said, the public would also be a lot safer if everyone had the grace and gravitas of Cynthia Portaro.

Dear Mrs. Portaro,

I know that I'm the last person that you would want to hear from, but I just wanted to tell you that I really am sorry for what I did, I'm not apologizing about what happened just because of the fact that I'm going to prison, but I'm apologizing because I hate to see the pain that I've caused, not only in your family, but in my family as well. There is absolutely no explanation or excuse for my actions, several words comes to mind but the one that sticks out the most is stupidity, I can't even began to imagine what you may think or how you may feel about me, but I hope that if you haven't already, that you will one day find it in your heart to forgive me, words cant bring your son back, and if I could give my own life to give him back to you then I swear I would, I've thought about what happened every single day, and although I'll have to carry this with me for the rest of my life, just knowing, that you and your family can finally move on with your lives with some what a little bit of peace of mind is all that really matters to me at this point, that and forgiveness, but I'm not going to take up anymore of your time, I just want you to know that I sincerely mean everything that I said and I really am sorry for everything, that you've been through.

Have a blessed and happy life Mrs. Portaro

It is Okay to not be Okay

Chapter 12

THE JOURNEY OF STAGES

"Turn to me and be gracious to me, for I am lonely and afflicted. Relieve the troubles of my heart and free me from my anguish." Psalm 25:16-17 NIV

Nobody is ever prepared to lose a loved one, especially tragically. Recovery happens on a day-by-day basis. Sometimes, we release it to God, but we keep a little string attached to it, and we don't fully surrender our pain. Like an invisible cape that captivates your memories, when the wind blows a certain way, it catches your heart and there's another breakdown and future's destroyed. No matter where you have been, or no matter how long this takes, it only belongs between you and God. Again ... the word recovery is something parents, who've lost a child, never really fully recover from ... we walk through it.

After reading multiple books from Pastors and Counselors, it is my belief and opinion, stages of grief are not in any kind or type of order. Yes, the feelings and emotions of trauma are there; however, no one goes through them the same. Our society believes in the stages, but what this does to an individual dealing with loss is, it criticizes the person, believing they are "not doing this right or in a timely manner." When people are told this is the healthy way through grief, it becomes confusing to the mind, body, soul and spirit. I believe this can bring on depression, because people do, and will, grieve differently. Just because someone numbers the stage, it does not make it personal to the one walking the journey of these stages. I have witnessed this on several occasions, from those dealing with such enormous grief and trauma.

Some professionals want to place people in a box and say this is the best way you can "move on." Well, quite frankly, I would not go to a professional who gives you the status quo of steps. Listed are types of grief a person may experience ... Shock, Depression, Loneliness, Anxiety, Loss of Hope, Loss of Faith, Guilt, Anger, Fear, Isolation, Confusion, Hopelessness, Wounded, Desperate, Shattered, and Feeling Stuck. Along with these listed, there are many more emotions people deal with; these are simply main findings of the journey.

When these steps are introduced, especially to a grief-stricken parent, we're told this is the order we should follow for healing. It is just untrue. Yes, all the emotions are there; however, "they" come in waves. Our brains can't handle any kind of order in the process of acceptance, because we will never, in our lifetime, accept that our child is gone. I have watched countless sermons and read books on this subject over the years. Hearing this quote by many has irritated me to no end ... "God will restore everything taken from you." I believe He will restore, but certainly, He is not going to send our children back to earth.

However, letting frustration go recently, God spoke to my heart and told me exactly this, "Cynthia, I have given you hope in eternity. Heaven is where you will be fully restored, with your family; who I am here with for now. You and your life are important to me, and I will fulfill every promise I have given you. Not only for you, on earth, but also in Heaven." WOW, when we think, now, of His promises, we can share the peace that surpasses all understanding. Remember, it has taken me nine years to receive this healing, even though today, I will always dearly miss our family in Heaven.

Although there is not a particular order, shock is definitely an emotion a grieving parent will experience, at first, hearing the news your child is gone and taken too soon. This explains why the definition of shock is ... impact, collision, shock; meaning a forceful, even violent, contact between two or more things. Impact may be used to imply contact between two things, at least one of which is impelled toward the other. Collision implies the coming together of two or more things, with such force that both, or all, are damaged, or their progress is severely impeded. Shock often denotes the effect produced by a collision and carries the suggestion of something that strikes, or hits, with the shattering, disruption or weakening effects of a collision, explosion or blow. The key definition here is, "totally shattered."

So, how many of you relate to feeling as if you were hit by a Mack truck, when your child entered Heaven. It is a collision of so many emotions and utter shock. These shattering after effects are disrupting the order, in which our lives should have been.

Denial is another emotion that will soon show it's face. It can become unhealthy, when it's not addressed. People do not want to face their grief ... who does? How many times have you said, or thought, "I can't believe they're gone!" Taking breaks from denial is not a bad thing to do. I would watch a movie or funny program, go out with friends, who would allow me to speak about my trauma, or I would take a walk and cry out to God, which is where I found a release of some emotional healing.

Avoiding grief can have harmful consequences on your journey. If the emotions are there, it's important not to totally hide from them. We shouldn't ever feel we have to face all these stages at once, either. Grieving stages mean allowing enough time to remember your losses and feel your pain, as well as embracing occasional opportunities to distract ourselves and regroup. This is what I call, "Walking through, what you will never get over!"

God gave us these emotions to get us through the seasons of grief. Having faith in Him doesn't change how we feel about this journey. It gives us hope that we will be together again, with our loved ones.

"You've kept track of my every toss and turn through the sleepless nights, each tear is entered in Your ledger, each ache is written in Your book." Psalm 56:8 (MSG)

In the materials I read after Mikey's death, everything continued to revolve around, "The Stages". Recently, God gave me the phrase, Separation Anxiety. As I prayed about it, thought long and hard about this subject, I began to recall when my son, Mikey, was two-years-old. We decided to have our children attend a pre-school, for a few hours a week. I will tell you, we certainly both experienced separation anxiety. He would scream for hours, as I sobbed, watching him, hidden from outside the classroom. Fortunately, he had a very kind and compassionate teacher, who would allow him to sit on her lap, while reading a story, or talking to the class. She was very good at engaging Mikey, with the other students. It took two months of this, every week, for us to adjust to being apart. Although our separation only lasted for a few hours, three days a week, it was torture.

Can you relate to this kind of torturous separation? Maybe when you took your child to their first day of kindergarten, the event can be a nightmare for some parents. How about when your first-born child graduates from high school and is now leaving the nest for college? I will never forget when our son, Rico, was in his senior year of high school, preparing to leave for college. I found myself sobbing, in the aisle, at The Party City Store, looking at invitations six months before his departure. The first few months, starting out in college, he called several times, stating he wanted to come home, because he missed his family. One time, I just said, heck with this, and bought him a plane ticket home, just for a short weekend, to connect with his Mommy and his family.

I never wanted to share the feelings a parent has, who is sending their child off to a military base, with the potential of serving in a war, uncertain if they will come home alive. Think about a puppy or kitten being taken from its warm, comfortable place, snuggled up against its Mommy's body, breastfeeding. When they're separated, they will cry and weep, until they are fed or held.

Now, just imagine a child dying for senseless reasons. Any time a child dies, no matter their age, it is a senseless death. To be separated by death, from your child, is the ultimate separation. Parents who suffer this loss feel like continually screaming out, because we are emotionally in constant pain, we can't sleep, we can't eat and so much more. I remember doing laundry one day, and I was home alone. I pulled clothes out of the dryer and there was a pair of Mikey's socks. I put those socks into my face and screamed out sounds that didn't even feel human.

After Mikey's and Chrissy's deaths, I would have thoughts I was going crazy at times, and I probably was. No one knew

106

what to say, what to do or how to act around me. There are those thoughts and feelings we never have been prepared to live through. So, with all this being said, I have added Separation Anxiety to the list of stages. Those parents reading this, who have lost a child, will most definitely understand this stage of such great loss.

On Valentine's Day, prior to Mikey's death, he bought Chrissy a cute little, red, stuffed Teddy Bear. She would sleep with it every single night. After he died, she hugged that little guy, like he actually was Mikey. As I wrote before, she would be holding this bear, crying, "I wanna go be with Mikey!" This may seem odd to you, then again, life is odd and so unpredictable. But, when Chrissy died, I seriously could not even imagine how I would be able to breathe again, let alone live. I wanted to check out. Somehow, I found comfort in hugging and holding that little, red Teddy Bear. At times, when I needed to cry out from the depths of my soul and spirit ... I found solace in this unusual way, especially as "a grown up."

I know it's kind of strange, but this little guy didn't tell me, "Don't cry." "Move on." "They're better off." "They're with Jesus." "You're so lucky to have two angels in Heaven."

No, this little guy just let me be. Be where I was. He filled an empty spot "no one" could fill. I still have that little guy. Although, I don't sleep with him any longer, he and a little lamb from Chrissy's childhood are sitting on my treasure chest, right next to my bed. The little things become important memories, as we move forward through this unimaginable journey.

Nothing comes easy in life that does not require a lot of work ... even grief. In my opinion, there are so many emotions walking through this journey including goodtimes, laughter, joy, hope, trust and redemption for our losses. God promises to restore us from our brokenness and heal our hearts from such devastation.

"I will strengthen Judah and save the tribes of Joseph. I will restore them, because I have compassion on them. They will be as though I had not rejected them; for I am the Lord their God and I will answer them." Zechariah 10:6

"I have seen their ways, but I will heal them; I will guide them and restore." Isaiah 57:18

If God "just" promised to restore us, it would mean He could help us make our lives what they always should have been. That's great, but there's still this journey of grief from everything we lost. I am a strong personality and don't like anyone telling me what "I need to do." If you have not lost a child, I am sorry, but you do not have the authority to speak into my life. I went to a Christian counselor about a month after Mikey was murdered ... asking me questions like, "How much time do you think you will need to counsel with me?" "Is your faith strong enough to move on rapidly?" I didn't have answers to any of those odd questions. So, I stood up and politely told her, "Thank you, I see you are not qualified to counsel me or my family."

So, I went home, cried, and said, "No one will ever get this pain I am feeling." After crying out to God, for what felt like hours, ... I decided to Google Christian Grief Counselors. The first in the search was Kimberly Malloy. After reading her bio, I called and left a message, with my name and number. She phoned me back a few hours later, and this is how our conversation went.

Kimberly ... "Hi Cynthia, this is Kimberly Malloy returning your call."

Me ... "Thank you, I appreciate the call back. I searched for a Grief Counselor on Google and your name was first on the list."

Kimberly ... "Cynthia, I know you. I have been praying for you and your entire family since Michael was murdered. We have mutual friends, and I am currently on staff at the ICLV (my church) Wellness Center."

Me ... "WOW that is amazing. Tell me, Kim, how is it you are qualified to counsel me and my family? What makes you a grief counselor? How do you counsel families that are dealing with trauma and Post Traumatic Stress?

Kimberly ... "My sister died tragically a few years ago; and after going through my own grief journey, I decided that I wanted to counsel those through such a devastating time."

Me ... "When can I see you?" I heard tenderness in her voice, who could counsel our family, with an understanding compassion.

I cannot begin to share with you how important it is to be able to counsel with another, who understands this kind of suffering. Kimberly brought me and my entire family through years of difficulty. She was also there for us when Chrissy died ... again tragically. We are all so grateful for the time, knowledge, and love she has given us. There is something about sharing your story and pain with another, who understands this journey. I was in awe of God and His goodness, to place such a gem of a professional, who walked us through this unbelievable time. After a time with our counseling, we started a support group together, at my church, to help those, who needed to have someone, anyone hear their story.

Also, after the death of Chrissy, a lady reached out to me, who I did not know. Her name is Karen. She shared with me how we had mutual friends and shared her story about the death of her 15-year-old son, Kyler, after a lengthy battle with cancer. Kyler and Chrissy were the same age. Talking with her, I felt like somebody else knew my pain and how our hearts connected was pretty incredible. Kyler was a soccer player and his number was 13 ... Chrissy's volleyball number was 13. To this day, nine years later, Karen and I have a bond of the heart, no one can touch. We encourage each other, we cry, we pray for each other and we reach out to others joining this "Suck Club." We also text each other every time we see 11:11 ... we actually do it a lot. I am so grateful to have friends like Karen, who took the risk to reach out, because this is something we should never have to do alone. She is why I made the decision to begin ministering to others, facing this incorrigible tragedy.

Then, there was my Mom, I call her Joan Jett. In 1979, my brother, Larry, died suddenly, at 26- years-old, from a brain aneurysm. All she was feeling was the loss of her son, now resurrected and amplified by the deaths of her grandchildren. Reliving this pain is a nightmare, and it's more than sorrowful to watch her try to remain strong for me, knowing how much she still longs for Larry in our lives. She is the grammar Queen of the universe and is currently editing much of my grammar for this book. We get to do this together, through the tears and laughter of all my mistakes and typos. I love her more than explainable, and I am so proud to call her Maaaaaaaaaaaaaaaaaaa!!!

Remember, you are wounded. Wounded people live in a protective state and sometimes shut out those who want to help. There will be a time you will be ready to take those band-aids off and allow some air in to breathe. The enemy targets the wounded ... please be aware of the thinking process of grief. It is definitely one of the most difficult battles to overcome, especially in the beginning stages of loss. It took me over a year and a half to put my head on my pillow and actually fall asleep, without thinking of all the trauma from my children's deaths. The deeper the wound, the more you will face this mental battle. Please protect yourself and do not allow negative or toxic people to tell you to "move on" or "get over it!" Our children are not an "it."

For a very long time, I would get out of bed, put on my slippers and say out loud, "Lord I am going to trust You to be there for me today." God is, and will always be, there any time we open our hearts to Him, for healing, guidance and restoration.

Where do you find emotional healing? Is it God or is it the god of substance? Many times, during my journey of day-to-day emotional anguish, people would offer me sedatives or marijuana, among other different things. Instead of turning to these methods, I made the choice to Fully Rely On God, or "FROG", to survive this mess.

I believe there comes a time when we need to enter into God's Emergency Room. If you need any type of surgery, where do you go? You find a doctor and listen to his wisdom to help correct the physical healing. Well, my friend, God is our emotional Physician, and He is carrying you through the trauma. Even when you can't feel Him, He is there. It takes daily decisions to trust He will heal your heart, that is in a thousand pieces. In Isaiah, he promised the Messiah would come to heal the brokenhearted.

"The Spirit of the Lord GOD is upon me, because the LORD has anointed me to bring good news to the poor; He has sent me to bind up the brokenhearted, to proclaim liberty to the captives, and the opening of the prison to those who are bound; to proclaim the year of the LORD's favor, and the day of vengeance of our God; to comfort all who mourn." Isaiah 61:1-2

No one should tell you the order of steps you will take, through this journey. There is no question, though, you will walk through them all. The choice is yours, to decide if you will be a victim or a victor and how you will use this trauma to walk through life. Do this in your own time and your own personal way. I do encourage you, again, please do not walk this alone. Please take care of your soul and choose to seek help. There are many people, around you, who will support you, encourage you and believe in you.

Reaching out to others is difficult at times, because when a new family joins this club, your heart breaks differently than it once did. It becomes very personal to us. Our mind and heart want to run from reliving these feelings of such brokenness. There actually is so much healing for you in the process, when you understand the heart of a grieving parent. Personally, for me, it's Moms and a few Dads ... reach out and touch those, who do not know where to turn ... it will touch you more than you will ever be able to conceive.

Personally, my belief, first, is to turn your troubles over to God. Secondly, allow those who understand what you are going through to walk alongside you. *"DO NOT ACT*

SO STRONG AND TRY TO FOOL PEOPLE INTO THINKING YOUR HANDLING THIS AMAZINGLY." God put so many people in my life, who understand this kind of trauma. I am so grateful to have the opportunity to bond to those who get this unimaginable pain and sorrow. Thirdly, allow yourself time to feel what you have endured. There is no time limit on grieving ... it truly is the price we pay, when we love someone so deeply. Especially your offspring.

———————

Prayer for You

Thank you, Father; for the courage You give us to reach out to families, who are hurting so deeply around us. Ministries come out of devastation, because You desire to heal those broken by such great loss. Show us how to be a beacon of light for others and encourage one another in our hopelessness. Help us to keep on growing in our small victories of healing. Thank you, for those You place in our lives to be a strong support, during this time of the healing process. We lift those up to you, beginning this journey, and ask You to comfort every ounce of their souls. We love You, and we believe in the power to overcome, with You carrying us through.

"My precious child, I love you and will never leave you, never ever, during your trials and testing. When you saw only one set of footprints, it was then that I carried you."
-From the poem, *Footprints in the Sand*

In Jesus Name, Amen, Amen and Amen!

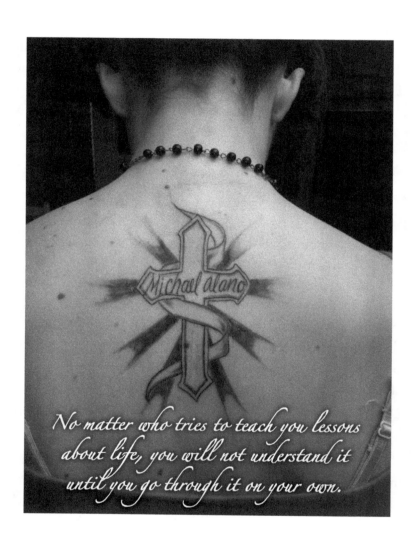

Chapter 13

I HAVE LEARNED

"My son, if you accept my word and store up my commands within you, turning your ear to wisdom and applying your heart to understanding, indeed if you call out for insight and cry aloud for understanding." Proverbs 2:1-3 NIV

I've gone through too much to let you simply read through these events, and then walk away, without a takeaway. Even with several counseling sessions, life became an emotional battlefield for our entire family. A battlefield that I am aware so many others end up facing, at some point in life. The battlefield of loss and grief.

Grief is not for anyone who thinks it comes without a battle, and a lot of hard work. Families are sometimes separated by the anger, hurt, and pain accompanying their grief. While one wants to talk about it, maybe get counsel, the other just wants to shut it out of their life and not deal with the brokenness. I personally know several who have divorced, after losing a child.

Rico and Joey didn't want to be in our home because of all the agonizing memories. Family dynamics are difficult enough, with seven different hormones in the household, then throw in the wrench of trauma and stuff blows up. Especially, since I was a picture person and had every year of their lives plastered all over the walls. My bathroom make-up nook was wallpapered with special pictures drawn, notes from the kids and those little sports buttons we wore, displaying our

115

incredible little babies in uniform. We had five kids, so there were a lot of torn and tattered memories on that wall. The kids would make sure I put up their proud creations, immediately after presenting their precious works of art.

The deaths of my two children has caused me to look deeply into my heart and soul, and reevaluate who I am. Not as a wife, mother, daughter, or friend, but as a "Child of God." The Bible speaks that our identity is in Christ, *"Before I formed you in the womb, I knew you, before you were born, I set you apart; I appointed you as a prophet to the nations." Jeremiah 1:5*

So then ... I must be appointed with a purpose!

As a young girl, all I aspired to be was a Mom, of many children. Most recently, I have reflected on motherhood, more than anything else. During this reflection, I began to realize how, in becoming a mother, I had lost myself as a person. Fortunately, I was able to be at home as Mom, with our children for many years, and I went full force into motherhood. If there were any activities involving our kids, I was there. Food preparer, taxi driver, cheerleader, PTA President, school volunteer, football Mom, volleyball Mom, basketball Mom, etc. I was known as Momma P at school. I knew everything that took place in their lives and what they and their friends were planning. We had them out volunteering for kids that are disabled, feeding the homeless, and so on, at very young ages. As far as we believed, it was our job as parents to raise strong, Christian, independent, kind, compassionate kids, along with stressing a good work ethic. Needless to say, we raised five children with heart and dedication, in a world where many have lost hope in our future generations. I am proud of the role model we provided, for our children, as parents. However, somewhere throughout the years, I lost sight of me, who Christ valued, and had many future plans for, outside of myself.

When the pain of losing our two children turned our lives upside down and then my husband passed away two years later, my identity was extremely more than challenged. I was left with so many thoughts and feelings of, "Who Am I?" The only place I knew where to turn was my Bible. I began a search, in what became time for me, to discover this question, which at some point will eventually surface.

Going from a household of seven to one, was unreal and confusing. My other grown children live on their own now, working and attending college. Learning to cook for one, this is not an easy task for a woman who loves to cook, and to this day, I have not mastered it ... AT ALL! I am constantly calling my kids to let them know there are plenty of leftovers.

In the loneliness, all I could do was empty my pain over to God on a daily basis. He began an interesting new process, through me, changing my mind and heart. In search of His plans to use this mess, of the loss of our two children, I believed there would be a message of hope for so many, dealing with trauma. When we allow Him to do His work, our identity becomes based on how God sees us. I didn't feel the need to find my worth anywhere else any longer. There is something in learning, we cannot heal alone. The saying, "It takes a village," became very real, as I walked through these incredibly difficult and tumultuous waves of grief, depression, and a lot of anxiety. Learning to allow people to bless me, during this time, was another lesson I had to learn. Strong, independent women like me, don't ask; we push away any help or opportunity for others to bless us.

Lesson learned: Cling to those who want to bless you. As it turned out, it's not so difficult to ask others for help, when you need it. If it is companionship, prayer, wise counsel, crying, or laughing together with someone, who loves you so much, to weather the storm, with arms wide open. Most people I found, who love God, are the people who have stuck by my side, even today, many years later.

Losing loved ones or experiencing traumatic events, in my case, both, do not come without expelling gut-wrenching tears. The same heartache is still there, as I relive the nightmares, while writing this book. I have learned that crying is not a weakness; it is a strength God gave us, to overcome weakness.

"But he said to me, "My grace is sufficient for you, for my power is made perfect in weakness." Therefore, I will boast all the more gladly about my weaknesses, so that Christ's power may rest on me. 10 That is why, for Christ's sake, I delight in weaknesses, in insults, in hardships, in persecutions, in difficulties. For when I am weak, then I am strong." 2 Corinthians 12:9-11 NIV

It is extremely difficult to search deep within your grieving soul, and share the pain that strikes you, in a moment's notice. It has taken me years of prayer, fasting, and revelations from God, to be strengthened into a state of letting go of uncertainties. There are times, it is easier to hold onto the pain. It becomes a fear of believing we will dishonor those who left us. People say "move on"; I say "move through those difficult waves." There are those uncertainties of where this suffering will take you, or how deeply it is going to hurt. Even through the entire journey, I had to choose to push myself continually, to make it one more minute, hour, day, month and year.

118

Where do you draw your identity from? It took me these past nine years to finally realize, I needed to stop looking at people, things, or outside worldly activities, and just allow God, to use my life, to possibly touch one other life, that is walking this journey, I call suck. "Really Sucks!"

I have also learned there is an unquestionable bond between parents, that have given their children back to God. In the almost nine years of tragically losing my kids and husband, I am in awe of the number of people I have now connected with and ministered to. God has given me a valuable ministry, that has now grown to more than 75 Moms. We were meeting at church, but it became too draining, emotionally. I now have formed groups of four to six women and we meet at a restaurant for Happy Hour. For me, it is now much more rewarding, because we are bonding amongst others, with the same heart condition. We cry a little and laugh a little and feel totally comfortable to talk about our children or spouses. It has been a blessing to watch Moms bond, creating new friendships. There is power and healing, when we connect with others who get this "Suck Club." It is a safe place, where we are not judged for being stuck in a particular spot, in our very own personal walk. These women have become true "Rock Stars" to our group of survivors, who will never, ever get over losing their children.

If you are someone who has lost someone you love, I would encourage you to seek groups or start your own. *Meet Up* online is a good place to begin. I also have **two Facebook sites where I share Godly perspectives toward healing: "A Time to Heal" and "Mourning Hope of Las Vegas".** *DO NOT DO THIS ALONE!*

Grieving parents understand, there is no getting over the death of our children; however, even in grief, there is hope, that joy will be part of the process. Grief and joy do coexist, depending on the day, the holiday, the memory, or whatever may strike you, at any given moment. Despite our losses, we are overcomers, who have our sights set high, to change the world and help a recent "Griever" walk the journey. Not only for them, but something within us, desires to honor the lives of those we lost, in order to make a difference and keep their memories alive. Many will agree, we would like to see a change in how people respond to us, and what to say, or do for us grievers.

Not long after my children died, I felt my heart muscle actually hurt. As if I had overworked my body muscles at the gym, it hurt that much. So much, I felt it was pounding out of my chest, and it awakened me in the middle of the night. There is a diagnosis for this and it is called **Broken Heart Syndrome. It is a temporary heart condition that is often brought on by stressful situations, such as the death of a loved one, a serious physical illness or surgery.** People with Broken Heart Syndrome may have sudden chest pain or think they're having a heart attack. During Broken Heart Syndrome, there is a temporary disruption of your heart's normal pumping function, in one area of the heart. The remainder of the heart functions normally or with even more forceful contractions. Broken Heart Syndrome may be caused by the heart's reaction, to a surge of stress hormones.

This was **published July 17, 2019 by WebMD**[3] ... **"Broken Heart Syndrome" may harm more than just the heart, new**

---

[3] https://www.webmd.com/heart-disease/can-you-die-broken-heart#1-2

research suggests. While the extreme stress of losing a loved one has been linked to heart troubles in prior research, a new study found that one in six people with Broken Heart Syndrome, also had cancer. Broken Heart Syndrome causes sudden, intense chest pain and shortness of breath, that can be mistaken for a heart attack. These symptoms are a reaction to a sudden surge in stress hormones, according to the American Heart Association (AHA). The condition causes the heart's main pumping chamber to enlarge, the researchers said. And, that means the heart can't pump blood effectively. Broken Heart Syndrome can happen, after just about any intensely emotional experience. The death of a loved one, a breakup, or divorce, financial problems, etc., can be related to cancer.

Again, turning to God for answers, He took me to *"May God himself, the God of Peace, sanctify you through and through. May your whole spirit, soul and body be kept blameless at the coming of our Lord Jesus Christ." 1 Thessalonians 5:23 NIV*

According to the Bible, mankind is distinct from all the rest of creation, including the animals, in that we are made in the image of God. As **God is three in one – Father, Son and Holy Spirit**, so then, **we are created with three parts: Body, Soul and Spirit.**

Humans are made up of physical material, the body, which can be seen and touched. However, we are also made up of immaterial dimensions, which are intangible; this includes the soul, spirit, intellect, will, emotions, conscience, and so on and so forth. These immaterial dimensions – spirit, soul, heart, conscience, mind and emotions – all makeup you. The Bible makes it clear, the soul and spirit are the primary immaterial dimensions of humanity, while the body is the physical container, that holds us all together.

When we are awe struck, with emotional pain, stressed or feeling overly fatigued, it may be your soul who is crying out for rest. As much as we want to escape the trauma, by overachieving and burying the reality this has happened, our soul needs rest, too. Your soul has to have time to heal, just as if you cut yourself, or broke a bone. If you do not allow yourself this time, there can be many physical consequences to your body. As with me, being diagnosed with colon cancer, seven months after Chrissy died.

Laughing again is okay, too. As difficult as it is when you feel guilty you smiled or laughed, it is okay. After Mikey entered Heaven, I thought no one in our family would be able to laugh or feel joy again. Chrissy had a laugh you'd have thought came from outer space, because it was so deep and loud. It was one of those laughs that made you laugh just because she was laughing so loud and hard, and you have no clue why you're even laughing. I did not hear that laugh again, until four months after Mikey's death, and I felt just a flicker of hope for us. For me, it was watching The Nanny reruns over and over again. I was sad when they took it off the air, because it was what made me laugh, forget my life and numb my pain. We also have our youngest son, Joey, who seriously can make you pee your pants with deep, you will cry, laughter. Whenever I am really feeling down, I FaceTime him and ask him to make me laugh, with his imitating multiple voices, improv comedy, dialogue, and uncanny humor.

Laughing releases endorphins from your brain, reduces the level of stress in your body, and strengthens the immune system. It is proven laughter therapy, also known as humor therapy, can reduce negativity, emotional stress and physical discomfort.

This is why I began writing this book. Not just for you, for me too. There is healing in writing, it's learning what our minds, bodies, souls and spirits are going through. It brings peace, discovering I can be a **Beacon of Hope**, through this journey, of life and death, which is part of our own personal recovery. One of a grieving parent's greatest fears is their children will be forgotten ... doing anything to honor their short life, will keep memories alive.

Ironically, while writing this chapter, I received word of three more childhood deaths, and I will now have to welcome other families to this *Suck Club*.

A Prayer for You!

Father in Heaven, I ask You to provide **Supernatural Strength** during the seasons of grief and weeping. Father, let those who are in this season, struck so tragically with life's greatest loss, find You in their mourning. Surround them with Your **Presence of Hope** in this hurting world and **Breathe Life into their Souls of Sorrow**. Give us the **Peace that Surpasses any Understanding** we have in us. Let **Faith Rule in our Hearts** and begin to heal every piece of what's missing. You are "close to the brokenhearted and those who are crushed in spirit." Psalm 34:18 (NIV)

"There is a time for everything, and a season for every activity under the heavens. "A time to weep and a time to laugh, and a time to mourn, and a time to dance." Ecclesiastes 3:4 (NIV)

Father, draw nearer to us, and lift us up and restore our hope in You once more. Help us to believe tomorrow will be better, the next day might be easier, and the day will come, when we will feel ready for what You are doing. Show us to have the faith for what we cannot see and where You will take us along this journey of such great loss.

In Jesus Name ... Amen

———————

"The length of time it takes getting over
losing someone only reflects the magnitude
of the loss...not the weakness of the
person experiencing it."
Ranata Suzuki

Chapter 14

EMOTIONAL ISOLATION

I decided to dedicate an entire chapter on this demon. Please be aware of emotional isolation, it will make you crazy and can lead to feelings of loneliness, depression, or anxiety. Sometimes, you even start over-thinking and believe no one would want to be around you, because of the emotional state you are going through. We were created to coexist with other humans, not be separated from others. This is especially important in times of deep emotional stress and grief. Yes, people will irritate us; however, we still need the source of comfort from others, who care deeply for us and our losses.

I have been guilty of isolating myself from those who wanted to help. Getting into a pity party can become very easy, when the rest of the world is moving on, and you're feeling like no one cares, or even remembers, your child died. Don't get me wrong, ... sometimes, being alone to sort out these overwhelming feelings can bring out personal growth. Just don't stay **stuck** there. Reach out to those, who you know, will always be there for you ... no matter what. Going without human contact for too long, can literally break your heart.

When I was feeling like running away from life and just wanted to be alone, I would study and learn about what I was feeling and how to overcome it. This short article below is something I came across and decided to challenge myself to fight this demon and overcome these feelings, because I did not want my children to see their mother in this state of loneliness, depression and oppression.

From the dawn of human civilization, we've relied on belonging and interaction with others to survive. Through evolutionary collaboration and cooperation, our "power in numbers" philosophy landed us right here: sitting on a posh couch cushion, scrolling through Instagram, and binge-streaming Netflix (instead of, well, fending off a bear). And we're probably feeling a little lonely.

People are hardwired to seek social structures to survive the brutality of nature. Still, it's safe to say most of us aren't at the mercy of nature anymore.

... Or, in some sense, aren't we?

Studies have shown that feeling lonely for too long may be directly correlated with the rapid development of mental illnesses, physical diseases, and overall brain deterioration. We need face-to-face human connection – something our current circumstances aren't providing much of.

It's crucial to note that we can't address the psychology of loneliness without also discussing its neurobiological side. If you've been feeling down in the dumps, you aren't strange – you're merely a shining example of a long-evolved biological mechanism.[4]

The loss of a child is, by far, one of the most difficult emotional states to overcome ... many of us understand the mental, physical and soul work it takes to walk this journey. A grieving parent can be in a room filled with people and still feel alone. It's easy to check out and feel like no one cares if

[4] https://www.hotelcaliforniabythesea.com/2020/03/26/ social-isolations-effects-on-mental-health/

I am even here. They're all laughing and having a good time, and I am stuck in this grief no one understands.

This can change, if you begin to change your mindset. People do care about you and what you're facing. More importantly ... God cares! I would search scripture to memorize, when feeling these negative thoughts and emotions. This, in particular, I keep embedded in my soul.

"So do not fear, for I am with you; do not be dismayed, for I am your God. I will strengthen you and help you; I will uphold you with my righteous right hand." Isaiah 41:10

I know most of you don't want to feel this way, but the inclination to stay in and stay away is stronger than ever, after the death of a loved one, especially the loss of a child. The shift caused by significant loss can lead you to feel more isolated than you're accustomed. While you try to adjust to life, in the wake of a major change, its business as usual for those around you. It is easy to feel cut off from family and friends, left out, alienated or misunderstood. Not to mention, many people intentionally isolate, due to feelings of anger, sadness, mistrust, helplessness, anxiety, and depression. Grief and loneliness go hand in hand, for a number of reasons, but I'll name just a few ...

Your friends stop calling, because they feel uncomfortable, and don't know what to say. You think they no longer want to be around you, because you're feeling sad and are uncomfortable if you're talking about your deceased children.

Your spouse has died and, everywhere you go, you feel like a third wheel, or just feel very awkward, showing up alone.

Every interaction you have is filled with those superficial, "I am so sorry for your loss."

You don't want to leave the house, because you're tired of having to reassure everyone you're doing okay.

You don't want to leave the house, because you're afraid something will trigger your grief and you'll become an emotional basket case, in public.

The things that used to seem important, now seem pretty petty and unimportant. People seem difficult to listen to, with their seemingly small trivial problems. You just don't care about much anymore.

You really do not want to be this way; you just want people to be compassionate about what you are enduring.

People are pushing you to feel better and you don't want to admit you are still in pain.

You don't want to admit you're lonely.

I could keep on, but you probably know, what I am writing is triggering some of those thoughts and feelings. The point is, for many reasons, grievers are at increased risk of experiencing social and emotional isolation and loneliness. For many, these feelings will be a temporary holding tank, but for many others, they could become habit-forming for constant negative thinking and actually withdraw.

For clarification's sake, I'd like to differentiate between social isolation, emotional isolation, and loneliness: Listed below was studied by the *American Psychological Association*

Social Isolation

According to a 2018 national survey by Cigna, loneliness levels have reached an all-time high, with nearly half of

20,000 U.S. adults reporting they sometimes or always feel alone. 40 percent of survey participants also reported they sometimes or always feel that their relationships are not meaningful and that they feel isolated.

Such numbers are alarming because of the health and mental health risks associated with loneliness. According to a meta-analysis – co-authored by Julianne Holt-Lunstad, PhD, a professor of psychology and neuroscience at Brigham Young University – lack of social connection heightens health risks, as much as smoking 15 cigarettes a day or having alcohol use disorder. She's also found that loneliness and social isolation are twice as harmful to physical and mental health as obesity (*Perspectives on Psychological Science, Vol. 10, No. 2, 2015*).

"There is robust evidence that social isolation and loneliness significantly increase risk for premature mortality, and the magnitude of the risk exceeds that of many leading health indicators," Holt¬Lunstad says.

This was something that I read in a blog, while searching these absolute must confront issues with such traumatic losses. I apologize for not remembering where I read it ... I had written it down a long time ago. I know myself and others share in these very real feelings of loneliness.

Emotional Isolation

When a person feels they have no one they can talk to or confide in. They sometimes have relationships that will trigger negative feelings and thoughts, so they withdraw as a defense against feeling stress, betrayal, pressure, shame or guilt. Emotionally-isolated grievers may get to a point, where they keep their feelings to themselves, and they feel totally despondent about communicating with others or receiving their emotional support.

For grievers, this might occur when they feel others aren't tolerant or accepting of their grief. They may also cut themselves off emotionally, if it seems like people are uncomfortable with their expression of grief-related emotions or if others react to their feelings in a way that minimizes their grief or pushes them to move on.

Loneliness

One's perception they don't have the amount or quality of social interaction they desire. The perception of feeling lonely is relative to what you feel would be personally fulfilling. Loneliness and isolation have the capacity to erode both your emotional and physical well-being. When you work up the courage to leave the house, you are more inclined to see the world through this negative lens.

As if the emotional toll wasn't enough, one only needs to research 'loneliness' to find that it's also linked to many physical warnings, such as, hardening of the arteries, high blood pressure, inflammation in the body, problems with learning and memory, lower immune system, increase in the stress hormone cortisol, quality of sleep and premature aging.

OMG! I'm grateful that I pushed myself to take a shower, get out of the house, and live my life, which was not over.

My counselor, Kimberly, shared this beautiful story. "I went to one of my favorite little home stores and was drawn towards an hourglass with sand. I picked it up and felt the Lord whisper, "Time. Pay attention to it."

I was like, Okay? I will make TIME one of my words for 2020, Lord. I bought an hourglass to serve as a reminder to me! Later, in my room, I felt the Lord impress on me, "You control how you spend your time, and I control when your time is up."

Truth? It was resonating in me, but I had no idea I would come face to face with the reality of this statement by the weekend. Truthfully, this may shift things for me. Don't mind me; if I say I love you more, and as a friend, I won't leave things unsaid, I will try not to leave things undone! This really struck my soul, to live with a passion, to serve and love beyond measure.

My counselor also suggested I submerge in warm baths. Bathing can diminish feelings of depression and pessimism, because it gives you a wonderful feeling of quiet and comfort. The feelings of closeness we receive from being submerged in warm liquid give us the comfort of being in the womb. Overall, bathing induces feelings of comfort and easiness, and that kind of security allows your mind, and subsequently your body, to relax. It can also help you sleep better and deeper. I use Lavender Epsom salts when I really need to chill and relax. Baths are also known to reduce blood pressure. By using heat to induce better blood flow and circulation, you're giving your body a mini-workout. It's also a great place to pray and even if you burst out crying ... it's a safe, warm, healing place to be.

Isolation is an actual health risk, so it's important to pay attention to how you're coping in the weeks and months following a loss, especially if you're someone who tends to withdraw from others. If you find yourself staying alone too long, it's probably time to find ways to connect. Here are a few suggestions:

- Get involved in a good Bible-based church. Find a place, when you walk in, you feel like you found home. Make sure the leaders are actually teaching Biblical principles from the Word of God. There are plenty out there, with support systems. Get to know people, in order to direct you to a good Bible study or group, for your needs.

- Recognize negative thinking and the stories you are telling yourself – "I'm not likeable, no one wants to spend time with me, everyone else is happy, everyone else has someone they can talk to, I don't fit in anywhere."

- Call a friend or someone you trust, who is a good listener, and go to lunch or dinner. Step out of your self-pity and accept an invitation to join a group or book club.

- Say hello, howdy, hi there, to a stranger. Smile at him or her and ask how they're day is going. It's amazing how people will open up about their lives. I met Anthony yesterday, what a wonderful spirit I found him to be. We shook hands after speaking and, as I said goodbye, I said, "May God Bless you abundantly."

- Find something to honor your loved one ... there are so many organizations that need you and your compassion to help others. If you feel like it's not a fit for you ... try another.

- Engage in conversations and question people about their story ... everyone has one. If you are human, you have endured hardship in this lifetime. Find a trustworthy therapist who understands trauma and grief. I prefer to recommend a Christian, who understands, our **Hope is in Eternity**.

- When I am really stressed out or feeling useless to society ... I clean. And ... I mean clean. Drawers, closets, garage, etc. Purging is good, when you're upset. There will be times you come across an item of your loved one ... tears are healing. Scream if you need to.

- Make the best of your time alone; do positive activities you enjoy. Invest in a massage, exercise, take a prayer walk, be there for a friend you know is experiencing difficulty; paint a wall in your home your favorite color ... not grey or black.

Your life is not over, until He brings you home. Carpe Diem is my daily quote. "Seize the Day!"

WRITE YOUR STORY!!!

A Prayer for You

Father, I pray for an increase of your love to surround those in need of healing. I pray, Father, in the Name of Jesus, you will be glorified through every loss, through every pain, and in all heartaches, they are facing. I ask You to strengthen those, who are weak, and that You would bind them to the Word of God and loosen the Spirits that keep them isolated from You. In our darkest times, being separated from You is something we don't want to face in the desperate times of needing You so much. Thank You, Father, that you are always with us for every open door and the ones You shut.

In Jesus Name!!! Amen

Faith is the strength by which a shattered world shall turn into light!!!

Chapter 15

SUPERNATURAL COURAGE

"Have I not commanded you? Be strong and courageous. Do not be afraid; do not be discouraged, for the LORD your God will be with you wherever you go." Joshua 1:9 (NIV)

Have you ever been amazed by someone who can do something out of the ordinary? Athletes achieving difficult tasks, people on stage speaking to crowds of thousands, Olympians performing miraculous, death-defying stunts, daredevils and magicians performing for a live audience. I believe you understand my point and have had those thoughts, "How'd they do that?"

It's not much different, when your life is turned upside down, and you are devastated beyond anything anyone can measure. It is where the heart comes to play, because it does not make any sense we are able or capable of what I've previously written, *"Walking through what you will never get over."* How does a parent live without their children present? I have learned your heart will take you places that your head finds inconceivable.

I can't tell you how to grieve, but I can share with you, who to grieve with. Christ is our only hope and strength during our time of trouble.

"The LORD is a refuge for the oppressed, a stronghold in times of trouble." Psalm 9:9 (NIV)

I have found, in my personal journey, most people believe in God, of course, in different ways. I find those that keep Him at a distance, only when trouble comes, they cry out to Him for answers. Yes, we all have questions we would like answered. However, if we truly know Christ and believe in His word, those answers are already written. We believe God loves us when life is going all good, but yet we blame Him for everything when life goes wrong. He's God, shouldn't everything be kept perfect, because we are believers. This went through my mind so much, it nearly drove me crazy; over-thinking I must have done something very wrong. "I mean why would He do this to me?"

As I cried out to God, those many dark times, "Why Me Lord?" God answered with, "Why Not You?" "Why them, Why others?" As I began to think of it, how is it we can live in this world of young people constantly dying, we turn our minds and hearts from it, because we don't want to hear or feel it? It is way too close to home.

When a friend's 23-year-old son passed, it was the first funeral I attended as a parent of teen children. "I have children that age." It's a thought no parent wants to accept when death hits close to home. I sat there frozen, thinking how sad to lose your baby. I couldn't even begin to imagine seeing one of my kids lying in a casket. I prayed for protection for my children, in most of my daily prayers, from then on. I have several journals with those prayers in them. I bet it just crossed your mind "well, prayers don't work then." It surely did cross mine. Continually, I questioned my faith throughout this journey of grief. Again, the question ... "Why Lord, did you not protect my children from such devastation?"

The answer is very simple "I don't know?" All I knew was I needed to Draw Nearer to My God, who loves me, delivers and gives us hope, in an uncertain world.

"May the God of hope fill you with all joy and peace as you trust in him, so that you may overflow with hope by the power of the Holy Spirit." Romans 15:13 (NIV)

You will never leave His presence, the same way you came, if you give Him all of "it". It is, "You and all your pain." If you ask, seek, and bang the door down, God will answer. He will give you a new strength and courage that exceeds your own capability. Then there will come a time when God will use you in a powerful way, and people will see, feel and touch the power of Jesus Christ.

In my lifetime, I could never explain the gut-wrenching cries and snot that came out of me. We moved just two months after Chrissy died. Going through both Mikey's and Chrissy's belongings was a very vivid nightmare. My friend, Priscilla, and I were sitting on Chrissy's bed, and all I remember were my guts coming out of my mouth. My stomach hurt for days after having to pack up their rooms. I did not realize in the beginning of my journey through this grief, God would use this mess to become a message of ministry. When you are willing to become His vessel of hope, even though we may not think we are qualified, *"Just being willing makes us qualified"*. When He is glorified through you, He will bring purpose to your pain.

I miss my family in Heaven so much, it hurts to no avail. When people lose someone they love, especially a child, grieving doesn't stop throughout the year. Some days are definitely easier, some more difficult. You'll hear a song, miss their laugh, have a memory, look at social media and miss their presence ... what should/could have been.

March 30, 2011, marks the day our lives changed forever ... the 364 days in the year are not much different, especially birthdays or holidays. It means the world to us, as a family, Mikey and Chrissy are always thought of in such a positive light. I pray each and every day they will continue to have an impact on people, as they both did, during their short lives. Every picture tells a story to me and, though we will not have the opportunity to have new ones, I treasure the ones, not only in my photo albums but, in my mind and heart as well. If, perhaps, this makes you shed a tear ... thank you ... it means you have compassion for a grieving heart and soul. Weaved in the pain of losing my children, I still found those beautiful memories as threads of hope.

I love my children more today and I am so very proud to call them my son and daughter. I thank God everyday He allowed me the privilege to love them and carry them within me every moment I live. They continue to inspire me, even today, as I look back at their lives and see what a testimony they have been to love and serve those who were lucky enough to know them. The way I choose to honor their lives is to always honor Christ first ... he died so that we may have life. Live that life to the fullest, with love, kindness, compassion and servanthood, to the person who, even though they might look good on the outside, ... you just never know what they are carrying on the inside of a broken heart. I feel blessed to share with you these past nine years of my journey for those who are reading my story.

"Man is least himself when he talks in his own person; give him a mask and he'll tell you the truth."- Oscar Wilde

Mikey had this quote tattooed on his arm. He was the kind of person, who was real and honest with you, and with himself. Mikey disliked any kind of controversy and was a peaceful, loving young man. He was funny ... but, was always true to his own person. Yes, of course, he had his weaknesses ... but, you knew what they were, because he did not hide behind a mask.

"Nothing in all creation is hidden from God. Everything is naked and exposed before his eyes, and he is the one to whom we are accountable." Hebrews 4:13

Is this not the truth when someone asks, "How are you?" We say, we're "Good, Fine, Comforted, Great ... etc." We wear the mask of grief, not allowing the truth to speak out of our broken hearts. Going through the grief process of loss is the most difficult of life's travels. The big question is how we proceed to do this and be our own person. There aren't many people who want to be around you, if you're a downer. Some days for me, right now, are like Halloween. Every day, I get up, shower, do my hair, then put on my mask of make-up. Every time I do this, I'm saying, "I am ok". I disguise myself as a normal person, who is coping well. At times, it's all a lie. Very few people know my disguise, even when they see me without make-up. It's tiring to lead a double life. I think I was meant for a life on the stage, because I've hidden painful times so well most believe ... "WOW... she's so strong, courageous and full of faith." Fact is, my disguise is beginning to fray around the edges and I was tired of wearing it. So, for those who understand what I am speaking of ... go ahead wear your mask ... but, allow those who want to pray, and encourage you through your pain, do that for you. I have learned to lean, not on my own understanding, but *"... trust in the Lord with my whole heart." Proverbs 3:5.* He places the exact people we need in our lives, when we need them the most.

In *James 5:16,* it says, *"Confess your faults to one another, and pray for one another, that you may be healed."* If people "think", we are doing okay, because we are portraying that to them ... then you won't be going through your pain in a healthy way. It would be your way. God says a clean heart puts you in a position to receive healing for yourself. *Psalms 51:10 "Create a clean heart in me, O God, and renew a faithful spirit within me."* It is through His Word and much prayer; we will be able to make it through the waves of grief. *"God is not a man that He would lie to us. What He says ... He will do?" Numbers 23:19*

"No word that has ever come from God can return to Him void." Isaiah 55:11. You can rest assured that whatever Scripture you are standing on for your healing contains enough power to bring about the manifestation you need. *Jeremiah 1:12 "I will hasten my Word to perform it."* Be assured God is watching over His word to perform His plans for your life.

So YES ... even through our pain we must live. Grief is something you may never forget ... but, you can get through it. Learn to be honest with certain people of Godly wisdom, and the people that love you ... you will be a witness to God's love and strength to get you through the days of pure utter hell. No one is without some form of "life" good, bad or ugly ... we will ALL have both. You have a choice, live alone in your pain or live it with those who will surround you with prayer and wisdom for strength you need to get to the good. Even in the bad, good will show up. You just have to look around; get out of yourself and recognize it. Allow Supernatural Courage to arise in you, allowing you to help someone else who is going through a difficult season. You will feel differently when you allow your heart to see people with so much love and compassion, it will transform you.

Shortly after Mikey's death, I had a dream he was much older, more mature. His eyes were a beautiful, sparkling blue that radiated the room, as they did when he was alive. We were standing next to a bed.

He spoke, "Mom I'm okay." He was writing something on the wall, showing me how he had already earned seven badges for teaching people to love. "That's my mission here Mom."

I asked him to sing me the song he wrote to me, when he was alive, I could not find.

He said, "Mom you have to let that go." Just then, he started writing the lyrics on the wall, "Mom you taught me how to be a family and how to love." He then hugged me so tightly; I did not want to let him go. He said, "Mom, I gotta go now. There are a lot of people that are in the other room."

I cried for him not to leave.

He hugged me really tight again and said, "I love you Mom, but you have to let me go now; there are people who need me. I am going to Australia."

He was so proud of himself and his mission God entrusted to him. I am not surprised, as that's the life he lived here. He loved so many people. The hundreds of cards and letters we received after his death displayed such love. I thank God, every day of my life, for Michael Alano, Mike, Mikey P; it is my joy and privilege to call him my "son".

I have doubts in what Christ will do for me and my living family. When I think or feel this way, I turn to Him and ask, "Where I have doubts, increase my trust in You." It's not about whether or not we believe some things we read, it's about having faith in The Written Word and how it speaks to us through the Holy Spirit. To believe in what we can't see is to have unwavering faith and when those mountains come, we have to climb. We will develop faith that is stronger, deeper and bolder than we could ever believe or imagine.

I used to say to my kids, "It just takes faith ... like the little mustard seed that grows into the largest of trees. Think of yourself as that little seed that is going to grow up big and strong ... like the tree." When Mikey was seven years old, he brought me an index card from school with three tiny mustard seeds taped to it ... I kept it on my car visor to remember what I had planted in their hearts as children. I found it after his death ... it became more valuable and more meaningful than imaginable. It's on my vision/prayer board now ... I can't tell you how many times I have touched those seeds, because it is all the faith I had on any given day. The seed of faith is in the condition of our hearts and the condition of the soil. Where the seed falls and is planted to grow. When our lives are so impacted with worldly things, sometimes we don't take time to allow the Word of God to grow in us. Taking time to be wrapped in His presence is something I had to develop with my busy working schedule.

144

"THE FIRST TO HELP YOU ARE THE ONES THAT KNOW THE INTENSITY OF GRIEF"

When life is going very wrong ...
take a moment to be grateful for
what God is doing all around you!!!

© Norina Leyde Photography

Chapter 16

BLESSINGS IN THE SUCK PART

C hildren are not supposed to die ... parents expect to see their children grow and mature. Ultimately, parents expect to die and leave their children behind. This is the natural course of life events, the life cycle continuing as it should. The loss of a child is the loss of innocence, the death of the most vulnerable and dependent. The death of a child signifies the loss of the future, of hopes, dreams of new strength and perfection. Those left don't get to take another picture, celebrate holidays, birthdays, graduations, weddings, or grandchildren. How does anyone not miss celebrating those most important of life's milestones or endure the sorrow of their relationship being gone forever?

I am sure anyone, who has lost a child, finds social media, at times, unbearable. Although, we do rejoice in families celebrating and sharing family photos, it really hurts deeply to see those milestones, and we are not able to share in the joy of it. Memories of our children, now in Heaven, is our "pain album", which reflects the challenges of life, with a deep abiding sadness. It's not that we choose to hang onto pain, it just hangs onto us. I am sure you will agree, we all have been awakened in the middle of the night, only to lie there with the rewind tape playing over and over again, with uninvited negative thoughts about our children being taken so soon and how they died so tragically. No matter what age a child is, it is extremely tragic to a parent and families who have lost a child.

146

It's difficult to explain the unexplainable to those who don't understand the pain we are hiding deep inside our wounded hearts. At times, it's nothing we can explain, as to how damaged and helpless we feel. We do hide it very well for those who do not "get us" and, believe me, we do not ever want anyone else to experience the tragic death of a child.

It's not uncommon for friends to pull away from you during this grieving season. It's sad, because they simply do not know what to say, and those who are parents probably feel uncomfortable with the reminder the loss of a child is possible. I listened to a Pastor speak on grieving, and he said, if it's been a year or more, it's time to move on ... "NOT!!!"

If anyone urges you to "Get Over" your grief and try to move it along, simply let them know that losing a child is something we never "Get Over." It is something we walk through for the rest of our lifetime. There absolutely is no timeline for this trauma. As I said, it has been nine years of maudlin memories for my family, who desperately desire all of our family here with us. We continue to feel, think, love and terribly miss those who died way too soon.

A week after Mikey died, Chrissy came to me and asked if I would take her to volleyball practice on the other side of town, about a 45-minute drive. I was shocked she wanted to go and even more shocked I said, "Yes." I was not showered and, in sweats, with a messy ponytail. Having time in the car with her was something I have always treasured because, oh, ... how she loved to talk. While sitting in the stands, watching practice, a lady came up to me and patted my knee and said, "Oh honey, I'm so sorry, you're just going to have to find your new normal."

As I went numb and checked out of what else she was babbling, all I could do was envision her plummeting down the stands and breaking her skull of stupidity. Whatever it was, I just wanted her to stop talking. When I retrieved back into her presence, I said, "What did you say?"

She said, "Well, you know, that's what they say."

I said, "I have no words, what a horrible thing to say!"

Especially, after a Mom is dealing with trauma a week after her son was murdered. For me, there was nothing normal about the brutal death of a child. I am sure she wanted to say something to comfort me ... but, really! You're already feeling numb with pain. There is no filter on how we may respond with what we are thinking. I have definitely become much gentler with responses to those who do not understand great loss.

So many people have good intentions, but saying meaningless words just doesn't do squat for a grieving person. This old one, "I'm so sorry, good thing they're in a better place." When a person is grieving, there is **NO** better place their loved one could be than at home with their family and friends, living life as it should be. We know where they are, but hearing it over and over is a bit much to handle. I also had someone say to me, how lucky I was to have two angels in Heaven. Shaking my head became a rather frequent ritual for me. I love to read, but I received enough books on death to wallpaper my entire home. Some encouraged me ... others, breezing through some of them, I found too sad to read so soon after the loss of our two children.

Surprisingly, our dear friends were those who were there to support our family. We had an army of people praying for us. Friends, and some people we didn't even know, scheduled daily meals; some even came to even clean our home. Linda, a neighbor from down the street became an instant friend to me. She owned a cleaning company and blessed us with free weekly service for almost four years. She shared with me how she had met Mikey for the first time through a mutual friend, about a month prior and, because he was so loving and jovial, she wanted to do something to honor him. WOW, God knew just how much this act of generosity would bless us in the upcoming months and years. I believe this was a divine appointment meeting Mikey. It definitely was not a chance meeting.

Richard came from a Catholic background, where viewing of the body in a casket is something traditional for them. As I said in a prior chapter, I would never be able to view my child lying in a casket. There are too many things you simply cannot unsee and I had seen enough. He decided he was going to go ahead as desired and have a viewing. Our children and I decided we would not attend the viewing service ... although Chrissy attended Mikey's.

After Chrissy's viewing, at a moment's notice, my dear friend Darlene, hosted a luncheon for a gathering of those who attended the viewing. We were able to spend time with a few close friends, and those we hadn't seen for a while, who wanted to share time, with our family. I felt very honored and loved by everyone, who took the time to be with us, just to show how deeply they cared for our family. There are so many things to be grateful for during those hardships we faced. We don't always see them, but God will reveal them when you're ready to receive them. However, as I look back at the friendships we've made in our lifetime, I will always treasure every single act of kindness. I have also been able to reciprocate as much as humanly possible, when those close to me have endured, not only the loss of a child, but other traumatic family losses.

I don't know who began the Michael Portaro reward fund. I do know our oldest daughter, Maressa, managed the Facebook page to help raise funds for a reward to find Mikey's killer, during the police investigations. I believe, at some point, they raised more than $30,000 and announced it on our local news channels, if anybody had information, they would receive this reward money. A gentleman we had just met a month before, personally donated $20,000. We will forever be grateful to Pat for his generosity and love for our family ... he continues to be part of our family today and has become best friends with our son Rico.

Mikey's longtime childhood friend, Megan, and her sister, April, who owns an ice cream shop, also had a community fundraiser to donate toward the reward fund. Another fundraiser was held at a specialty bakery shop, again organized by people we did not know. They all made special signs for these events, with a big beautiful picture of Mikey. All I have to say right now is my heart remains full, with gratefulness I will treasure forever.

Our sweet friends, Joan and Jim, hosted memorial dinners at their home, after both kids' Celebration of Life services. And, there were more than a few people who came to celebrate our kids' lives with us. Maybe, 4 or 5 hundred, I'm not exactly sure ... but it was such an overwhelming act of love for our family.

People rallied to help, give, donate money, serve food and drinks, create picture poster boards and special T-Shirts, for both kids. I am not talking a few hundred. More than a thousand for both of our kids, I believe some of the cost was donated by the company. My most energetic friend Chris was behind making sure they were distributed and sold at school for more fundraising. I can't even begin to explain how loved and grateful we felt from their school, Faith Lutheran, and the Las Vegas Community.

Our longtime friends, Vicky and Steve Quinn, invited us to join them during the summer, after Mikey's death, for a much-needed beach get-away. I was able to spend some quality time writing and enjoying hearing my daughter's vigorous laugh, for the first time in about four months. This time is something I will always cherish, never believing in just another month she'd be gone.

We were offered beach getaways, gift cards for evenings out, written testimonies from parents, friends and young children as to how Mikey and Chrissy made an incredible impact on their lives. Longtime friends, Alan and Christine, who owned a printing company, made all of our memorial cards and introduction pamphlets. There was nothing little in every act of loving kindness. Some who did things; I probably don't know about or remember. How does anyone repay those kinds of blessings, from so many gracious people, and many we didn't even know?

When I think about the many generosities and the love shown to us, it is unbelievable in those cold, dark hours in this world, people do shine a bright light during the dark times. I look back now and realize how much God was there, with us, providing the peace we needed. It was as if a galaxy of angels were hovering over us, throughout those extremely tough days.

I am so grateful for those God surrounded our family with during these most difficult times. Particularly, Rita Demilio,

I call Momma Rita, who continually prays for me and encourages me to keep believing and press on with writing this book.

Then, there were those after the aftermaths; those that stuck closer than a brother to do just about anything for us. We had several friends, who called or texted, to check on, us asking questions. "What do you need? "How can I help?" "Let me help!" Some would just pray for me over the phone and listen to me sob. Or, like my friend Laura, came right over to our house after I wasn't answering her calls. She literally took my clothes off and showered me. We recently laughed about it, not too long ago, as to how much of a Zombie I was. But I am sure, at the time, I appreciated it ... along with a good teeth-brushing.

After my behavior on Aspen Road, trying to grab the police officer's gun, my family and friends were concerned I might attempt to take my life. So, my husband appointed my most loving friend, Jackie who was there on Aspen Road, to sleep by my side every night. I remember waking up to her in the morning, feeling extremely cared for and loved. She really loved my kids and always welcomed us, as family, in their home. She is Aunt Jackie to my kids.

My very dear friend, Kimmy, who is also my hairdresser, showed up at my house before the Celebration of Life services to do my hair. She said, "No way am I allowing my girl to show up anywhere, unless your hair is perfect." To this day, she keeps my hair looking perfect.

My Mom, heartbroken and feeling there was nothing she could do for us, was always there by our side. She took a lot of time to care for our family. Making sure we ate, or just sitting with me crying, understanding the grief of losing her own child, my brother, at such a young age. She's always been my rock and what I inspired to be in life. A Giver!

I will never forget my close friends, Mary Jo, Jackie, Rick and Berta, who were there with me on that cold, dark road, where my baby lied, for hours. Then, there were my friends, Mark and Desiree, who stayed with Chrissy's lifeless, cold body, until the morgue took her away. It was dark, and in the mountains, there are many bugs at night. They said to the police, "WE ARE NOT LEAVING HER." This is a display of love at its best.

Christy, the director of the Las Vegas Funeral Home, where we had our children prepared for the viewings and cremated, was in Brian Head, UT, when she heard of Chrissy's accident. I did not find out until much later, she personally drove down to Cedar City, UT, where they had taken her body and personally brought her home to Las Vegas. She later told me, she walked into the hospital and said, "This one's mine guys. I'm taking her home where she belongs."

Tears are welling up inside me, as I write this memory of just how much God was always there for us, behind the scenes, making every perfect move.

We also received many letters about how our children made an impact on their lives. These came from teachers, friends, coaches, parents and people, who had heard of them through others. These gestures of such kindness blesses the grieving, when you hear from the community how someone you love so deeply affected their lives.

"Mike was one of those people that cared about everyone and was a very kind young man. I have never seen

him be unkind to anyone, when he wakes up, he wakes up kind." Judi Young

This came from a friend of Mikey's. **Dear Portaro Family, "I can't explain how great of an influence you and Mikey all made in my life. Mikey was the kindest, nicest, least judgmental man I have ever met! He always tried to use the values your family taught him. I am so proud to have known him and having you all take me in as a son during a huge turning point in my life. I love you all more than you know. You are the most inspiring family I know." Love Harper**

The entire school, especially Chrissy's graduating Class of 2013, donated funds to create a stone bench, outside The Chapel of Performing Arts, dedicated to Christina. It has her name, dates and volleyball with her #13 engraved on it. This is absolutely priceless to our family. I visit that bench all the time, just to sit and pray.

We had an influx of letters and testimonies written of how Chrissy touched lives. Her entire school at Faith Lutheran embraced us and took care of so many different responsibilities. The following volleyball game scheduled the "Friday Night" after her death, not one player wanted to play. They all said they felt guilty, as if they shouldn't play out of respect for their teammate. My husband, Richard, while we were still in Brian Head, UT, scheduled a conference call with the team and the coaches and said, "Girls, we've just got to do this. You have to ask yourself, what would Chris want us to do? You know what she would say; now go out there and kick somebody's butt!" ... they agreed, with heavy hearts, determined to honor the life of their teammate.

Chrissy's presence was terribly missed, not only by the team, but the entire school and community. More than a thousand people showed up for the game, wearing "Chrissy P" T-shirts, including us, as a family, to support the decision to play.

The Las Vegas Review Journal Daily Newspaper dedicated an entire page, with a picture of the girls wearing black socks that had CP#13 on them. And, with their arms around one another in a huddle, they jumped up and down together, shouting, "Chrissy P! Chrissy P! Chrissy P! Chrissy P!"

The entire opponent's team, Shadow Ridge, also wore black armbands that read "CP#13," prompting Faith Lutheran's coach, Amy Fisher, to call the Shadow Ridge players and coaches a "Class Act."

Before the game, Richard went into the locker room to inspire the team, before they took the court. "I'm not telling you that you've got to win this for Chris, but you've got to play hard for Chrissy and yourself. As long as you can say ... I left everything on the court, I gave it my all. And then, I personally want to look at every single one of you, check your arms and your elbows, and if you don't have scrapes on them, it's going to piss me off." That last bit got them laughing, something they all really needed.

I can't tell you this was not difficult to sit through, constantly looking for her #13. She was a beast to be reckoned with on the court as "middle", and she was intense with her hits; usually diving wherever the ball was headed. What made it even more difficult was driving home afterward, without Chrissy ... I don't even remember the ride or even much of the game. A lot of what I am writing is from friends and family, who shared these memories or from my journals.

After my husband, Richard, passed, I didn't know how I would ever be able to help my youngest son, Joey, stay in college. Our friends, Don and Lori, invited me, Joey, and his now fiancé, Kellie, over to their home. We chatted for a while, then Don spoke of how he and Lori wanted to pay for Joey's college tuition. It is very difficult to explain how I felt, as a mother, other than tell you all I could do was cry. I think it took the three of us a good 15 minutes to shut our surprised, speechless mouths. It is very amazing how God will show up, place the right people in your lives and handle every need you have.

As a family, we will forever treasure how family, friends, and the community of people rallied to honor our son and daughter. The compassion shown is what makes us driven to serve. These are the acts of human kindnesses that bless those in their intense moments of incredible pain.

And ... that's just about it. What you can do when a family is faced with tragedy. Love them, if you have something to give ... give it, if you can send a loving card ... send it, if you cook ... prepare a meal ... if you are financially capable ... donate. If you have the gift of prayer ... pray. It's no different than we teach our children growing up; it's not what you say to them, it's by the example we set.

I believe, as a community, we need to get back to a place who takes care of people through their tough times. Everyone is so busy; we all can lose sight of what's really important. Yes, life goes on, but even during the times of sorrow, it's important to know there is a community out there that cares.

In the Bible, depending on the version, the word "love" occurs 310 times in NIV, 280 verses KJV.

"Love the Lord your God with all your heart and with all your soul and with all your mind and with all your strength. The second is this: 'Love your neighbor as yourself.' There is no commandment greater than these." Mark 12:30-31

It took me eight years to give my children freely back to God! The ocean where our family loved so much and seemed the most real where He leaves His footprints in the sand. "Dust Thou Art ... Dust Shalt Thou Return" Letting go of what will forever be in my heart and soul is an act of willingness to allow Him to heal me. The depth of my hurt does not define whom God made me in Christ or where I am headed.

World here I come ... watch out ... and see what He will do ... in and through me.

May my journey strengthen you ... Cynthia Portaro

Chapter 17

VICTORIES

"For the LORD your God goes with you to fight on your behalf against your enemies to give you victory." Deuteronomy 20:4

According to His word, we are no longer defined by the wreckage our lives have been through. When you walk in victory, over feelings, it changes the atmosphere all around you. Please understand this does not come soon after the loss of a child, but **there is hope** in His plans for our lives. Here, I stand today, nine years later, I still think about my kids every single day. However, with the guidance of the Holy Spirit through these years, I believe in His power to restore life, just in a much different way and plan. Think of a GPS, it will reroute when there are obstacles in the way or you make a wrong turn. So, with God, He doesn't cause these senseless deaths, but He will redirect our steps.

I have always valued mornings with God. I grab a cup of coffee, read devotions and spend time with God. Before I meet with people, I need my God time. Do circumstances get in the way, absolutely. But, in these crazy times, a good daily filling of the Holy Spirit is necessary. Thankfully, I have always written my time with His still quiet voice speaking to my heart. It helps to look back what was written and see how far I have come along this very difficult journey. Time seems to be speeding up so quickly. During quiet moments, in His presence, you will have victories in all areas of your life. Even tiny ones are as important as the big ones. When I couldn't utter a word of prayer out of my mouth, I would just turn on worship music and lift my hands and surrender every emotion and those painful thoughts.

The anniversaries of firsts are extremely difficult times, not only for parents, but siblings, other family members, and friends. Please remember to rest. Your soul needs to rest. Emotional stress from trauma causes physical tiredness. Some will recommend that you get busy ... I began back to work three weeks after Mikey died. But, I have learned from experience, I did not take the quality time needed to heal. Which, I believe, was a major factor in my cancer diagnosis. Your body is in a sensitive, stressed state, and it can be affected physically by your emotional imbalance.

We normally spend much of our time, as parents, serving our families. I have a servant's heart and love to do so. It is a gift from God, to be treasured. However, I needed to learn to take care of myself or I would not be of any good to anyone else. Besides being constantly exhausted, due to keeping so busy and lack of sleeping well, I don't remember ever being able to think very clearly. Allow yourself a few bouts of tears. God gave us those tears, to release pent up emotional pain and begin the healing process. Try not to be so hard on yourself and let others know you need time to process and heal. My counselor told me it's ok to cry in front of your children and others. I thought I was protecting them, by hiding behind my facade, when actually, I wasn't teaching them it's okay to grieve ... not bury those ugly feelings. It took my oldest son Rico, over eight years, before he would talk about his Dad, brother, and sister. Unbelievably, Rico asked me if I would have a beer with him, to celebrate Mikey's 31st birthday. This was a tradition Mikey and Rico had, to celebrate with each other, on their birthdays. It was the first time since Mikey's death Rico decided to pick the tradition back up. We met up with Joey and his future wife, Kellie. I felt a special joy, as Rico began sharing stories of the younger days with Mikey.

No matter what you are going through or what you have been through ... Praise Him anyway. There is an unending joy that creates breakthroughs, when you can praise and give thanks and honor to our God, for what we cannot see all He is doing in our deepest, darkest moments.

"Praise the Lord. Praise God in his sanctuary; praise him in his mighty heavens. Praise him for his acts of power; praise him for his surpassing greatness. Praise him with the sounding of the trumpet, praise him with the harp and lyre, praise him with timbrel and dancing, praise him with the strings and pipe, praise him with the clash of cymbals, praise him with resounding cymbals. Let everything that has breath praise the Lord. Praise the Lord." Psalms 150:1-6 NIV

I have been told I have an unprecedented, childlike faith. No matter the circumstances, believe there is a God providing every need you have, before you even think about something. For me, there is no sea that can't be parted and no mountain will stand in the way. But it will take time and endurance, along with a whole lot of faith. When I travel, before getting on the freeway, I ask God to do what he did for Moses, "Yes", part the traffic. I can't begin to tell you, during California rush hour traffic, how many times my friends were shaking their heads as to why we didn't run into a lick of LA traffic ... as I would smirk, with a smile, up to the heavens.

My mother used to tell me, as a young girl, I could fall in a pig pen and come out smelling like roses. To this day, I believe, we don't have to stay in the pooping part of life. We can choose to make the best out of this journey. The thought process is the most difficult task of the how, to replace those dreadful thoughts we face in our brains. It almost requires a lot of brainwashing. As the Bible says, *"Take every thought captive."* Easier said than done ... it truly becomes a battlefield of the mind. Choose to use this battle for a greater cause. Find somewhere to serve your gifts and talents to those less fortunate. There is always going to be someone in life, who has it so much worse, than we do. After the loss of my children, I read of a wife whose husband and three children were killed in a small plane crash. I remember thinking, "How is she going to live through this?" Then I thought, "Oh, yeah exactly the same way I will."

There comes a time in life, when you should choose to walk away from any drama and people who create it. And ... they will come around. Remember, you are wounded. People will prey on your emotional state and then discard you, as if you never existed. Do not bury those gut feelings, you know those who really are wolves, living in sheep's clothing. Surround yourself with those who make you laugh, show you love, honor you and who are respectful of where you are in this season. Forget the bad ones, and focus on the good. Be with those who treat you right, pray for the ones who don't. Life is way too short and tomorrow is not a guarantee, so do something that makes you happy. No matter what we are facing, there will be those moments, we will truly be grateful for what we have and have gone through. Unfortunately, those difficult seasons are when we grow the most. Falling down is a part of life, getting back up is living.

Many ask where we can gain the strength to live and love again.

"What a wonderful God we have – He is the Father of our Lord Jesus Christ the source of every mercy and the One who so wonderfully comforts and strengthens us in our hardships and trials. And why does He do this? So, when others are troubled, needing our sympathy and encouragement, we can pass on to them the same help and comfort God has given us. Praise be to the God and Father of our Lord Jesus Christ, the Father of compassion and the God of all comfort, who comforts us in all our troubles, so that we can comfort those in any trouble with the comfort we ourselves receive from God. For just as we share abundantly in the sufferings of Christ, so also our comfort abounds through Christ. If we are distressed, it is for your comfort and salvation; if we are comforted, it is for your comfort, which produces in you patient endurance of the same sufferings we suffer. And our hope for you is firm, because we know that just as you share in our sufferings, so also you share in our comfort."
2 Corinthians 1:3-7

It is normal for me to ask God, throughout my day, to schedule divine appointments for me, in ways I would know, could only be from Him. One evening, my Mom and I were watching a movie around 8:30 p.m. We were at our condominium, in Brian Head, UT, for the week of New Year's, 2019. And, to our surprise, the doorbell rang. Of course, I answered it. There was a lady I did not know apparently, pretty shook up. She apologized for abruptly coming over. I told her no worries and asked if she was okay. She said, a neighbor had told her about me, and she should try to locate me. Apparently, she had seen the lights were on, and she took a chance, I would be there. I invited her in, as she was visibly upset. She informed me, her 32-year-old son had died suddenly, two years prior. I immediately embraced her and just allowed her to cry, as long as she needed. As I looked up to our God and smiled, I thanked Him for this encounter. I said to myself ... only You could set this up. We spoke for about an hour, before I handed her a manuscript copy of this book. She actually read the entire book that evening before falling asleep. We spent another couple of hours talking the next day, praying and sharing our testimonies. I felt so honored God would use me at the very moment, when she felt alone and had no one to speak to about the trauma of losing her son. We've kept in touch via texting, encouraging each other and thankful for the bond we share.

Just one week after this encounter, I traveled to California to move my mother to Las Vegas. After working at packing her belongings all day, I said, "Let's go to the California Grill and eat, I am starving."

We sat at the bar for Happy Hour, ordered our food, and were chatting. A gentleman sat one chair away from me; I looked at him and smiled. Something in my spirit told me to ask him how his day was.

He gave me an irritated look and said, "Fine."

I apologized for interrupting him and turned away, talking to my Mom. Then, there went that nagging Spirit, again, "Talk to him." I was like, "God, he apparently doesn't want to be bothered." The nudging was so strong, I conceded and calmly asked him, "Are you okay?"

He looked at me kind of funny and said, "Are you one of those physics?"

I laughed and said, "Kinda, God speaks to me!" I wasn't sure if he was going to hit me or run out the door. So, I introduced myself and boldly said, "What's wrong?"

He stared at me as if I were from Mars, and then very quietly said to me, "I found my 19-year-old son hanging from a belt in my home a year ago today. There are days I just need to be alone and grab a cocktail."

I told him, I totally understood and shared a little of my story. We exchanged numbers and I am sending him a copy of this book.

I share these encounters, because if you allow God to use you in unimaginable ways ... He will. These encounters happen even more often than I can explain to you right now. It blesses me more than anything to share the love of God, with those who are hurting, after such devastation. He will use you, too, if you open your heart to show you His healing power. It allows me to feel I am not only honoring God, but my children, too. There is healing in this journey, and you can push yourself through the pain. It just takes your daily decision to let Him carry you through, if only just that day.

I am looking forward to the year ahead. Can you believe it's 2020? I like to look up my dream interpretations and Biblical meanings of numbers. The number 20 is associated with a trial, a period of waiting and is successfully completed. The reward is generous and full of God's love. It also symbolizes the cycles of completeness. It's connected to a perfect period of waiting, labor and suffering, that is compared to a trial and now rewarded. I am claiming this for my life and for yours too. We can, and will, survive with our deepest hope in Christ.

He is there waiting for each and every one of us. He will never leave you or forsake you.

My Prayer for You ...

Today, May there be peace within. May you trust God, who has you exactly where you are meant to be. May you not forget the infinite possibilities that are born of faith, in His plans, for your future. May you use the gifts that you have received and pass on the love that has been given to you. May you be content with yourself, just where you are, and continually strive to be the best you can be. Let this knowledge settle into your bones and allow your soul the freedom to sing, dance, praise and above all love.

In Jesus Name ... Amen

Just breathe ... Victories are on the horizon!!!

ACKNOWLEDGEMENTS

God gave me an analogy of a strong and beautiful, tall tree. Some of the older branches were dry, cracked and will hurt you, if you brush up against them, while some were sprouting green leaves or even flowers. The dry ones break off or just hang there, until they are broken by hands that see it's draining the branches that have life and are flourishing. When different seasons come, the leaves and flowers blossom, as well as when the time comes for them to drop and fall to the ground. The roots of the tree could have hundreds of branches and leaves, but it takes just a few unseen roots to make sure the tree gets everything it needs to nourish itself.

I say this, because so many people will come in and out of your life for a season and for a reason. I thank God daily for the family and friends that have inspired, encouraged, prayed, and wept with me and counseled me through the most traumatic season a mother and family could ever imagine. "These people, I call, "my roots." If you have two or three people in your life that are grounded and rooted in the Word of God ... it's life's greatest blessing. They show the amazing compassion of Christ for those that are broken and need time to mend. I personally thank these special influences, during this time of enduring which I call ...

"Something you will never get over ... but, will walk through."

If I could name every one of you, who have been there for me, I would. My heart would be broken, if I forgot to mention just one person, so I choose to just acknowledge "you" for watering my spirit, so that together we may minister to the lost, the hurting, the mourning, the grieving, and most of all, those who are going through the season called suffering.

When tragedy strikes you ... you can't help but make the shift of a drastic change in your life. It is an inevitable destiny; it has no control or boundaries. It takes you deeper into your soul and spirit than you have ever imagined. Thankfully, there will always be The Savior, to carry you through the journey, until we draw our last breath.

"The first to help you are the ones that know the intensity of grief."

All of My Deep Love For "You" and Forever Grateful

Cynthia

ABOUT THE AUTHOR

Cynthia has been a born-again, Spirit Lead Christian since July of 1988. Their son, Michael, was hospitalized at six weeks old with a heart defect, involving a narrowing of the main aorta, known as a coarctation of the main aorta. It was then, she made her promise to God to raise and influence her children to know Him, if He would spare little Mikey's life. A lot of bargaining went on for his life to be spared. At a very small chapel across from UCLA Hospital, Cynthia and her husband, Richard, gave their lives to live out His plans and promises for their family.

She and Richard raised five children, Maressa, Rico, Michael, Joseph and Christina. Maressa has three children, Braden, Brenna and Briley.

She is known by many of her children's friends in Las Vegas as Momma P ... and still has very solid relationships with many of those kids she refers to as sons and daughters.

She owns and operates a very successful Interior Design business in Las Vegas, NV. It's named perfectly, Cynsational, Inc. She has an intense passion for her work to create ultimate satisfaction and happiness for her clients. She strives to hear them walk into their renovated space and say ... *"WOW, I love it!!!"*

March 30, 2011, the family's lives changed forever, when the police came to their home at 3:30 a.m., and announced their 22-year-old son, Michael, had been shot and killed. Her faith did not waiver, but her life certainly did.

September 3, 2011, her 16-year-old daughter, Christina, was tragically killed, while riding a four-wheeler, at their UT Mountain home. Cynthia arrived on the scene of the accident to witness and hold her baby's lifeless body.

April 23, 2012, Cynthia was diagnosed with stage four colon cancer and was told she had six months to live. After surgery, and a lengthy pain riddled battle, she lives today to share her story of Faith, Hope, Inner Strength, Awareness and Encouragement.

October 10, 2012, Richard informed her that he was diagnosed with Squamous cell Carcinoma. This is the most common type of nasal cavity and Paranasal Sinus Cancer. After two surgeries and many different treatments, Richard entered heaven on Thanksgiving evening, November 27, 2014 at 11:11 p.m.

February 12, 2015, Cynthia, family and friends sat through 10 grueling days of her son's murder trial. There are things in this world you cannot unsee ... this emotional battle was one of them.

One would question Cynthia, as to how she has been able to walk this journey of trauma, in this short period, and her only answer has been,

"By the Grace of God ... I walk!"